FOLLOWING GOD'S BREADCRUMBS

Also by Elizabeth J. Harris, MSW

Forthcoming

Published by Elizabeth J. Harris, MSW

St. Louis, Missouri

www.followinggodsbreadcrumbs.org

ISBN: 979-8-9954856-1-2 (Hardcover)
ISBN: 979-8-9954856-0-5 (Paperback)
ISBN: 979-8-9954856-2-9 (eBook)

Library of Congress Control Number: 2026908143

Scripture quotations are taken from the Holy Bible, New International Version®, NIV® Copyright © 1973, 1978, 1984, 2011 by Biblica, Inc.® Used by permission. All rights reserved worldwide.

The names and identifying details of some individuals mentioned in this book have been changed to protect their privacy.

Cynthy's Kids, Inc. is a registered nonprofit organization incorporated in the State of Missouri on February 17, 2026.

Excerpts from the writings of Cynthia Elaine Davenport are used with the love and permission of her family.

Cover design by Elizabeth J. Harris, MSW

Interior design and typesetting by Hmdpublishing

First Edition

Printed in the United States of America

For information about bulk purchases, speaking engagements, or Cynthy's Kids, Inc., please visit www.followinggodsbreadcrumbs.org or contact LizHarris@CynthysKidsInc.org.

FOLLOWING GOD'S BREADCRUMBS

Out of Darkness and Into Purpose

Elizabeth J. Harris, MSW
St. Louis, Missouri

DEDICATION

This book is dedicated to the roots that support me and the wings that allow me to fly.

To my mother, Cynthia Elaine Davenport: Who birthed me twice. You were my primary architect. Thank you for teaching me that the "Why me?" of trauma is merely a vote of confidence from God. Your journals and your voice are the heartbeat of these pages.

To my grandmother, Joan DeFrance: My counselor, my guardian, my sounding board—one of the two women who were my biggest cheerleaders for most of my life. Thank you for the foundation of love that allowed me to eventually look up at the stars and see my own potential. You and Mom are back together now. I hope you know how much I still feel you both.

To my husband, DuJuan Harris: You arrived at that hospital in Albuquerque and didn't take the "out" I offered. Thank you for seeing the woman I was becoming when I couldn't recognize my own reflection, and for giving me the room to grow out of the cocoon into the butterfly God intended.

To my daughters, Elise and Madelyn Harris: You are the reason I put on my oxygen mask first. This work is my gift to you, so that you may walk into your futures unburdened by the "ice blocks" of the past. Your Mommy C wrote you a letter in 2016 and told you that you are divine originals—perfectly perfect, destined for greatness, with everything you need already inside you. She was right. This book is proof that her words were true—and that they were always meant to find their way to you.

To my brother, Joseph "Joe" Davenport: For being part of the story from the beginning and standing with me as we navigated the shifting landscapes of our family. It's you and me — the original Cynthy's Kids. Let's go show the world the type of children that she raised.

To my Father, Rev. Dr. Donald C. Davenport: For the "gems" of wisdom you placed in my path. Thank you for helping me realize that we all do the best we can with the resources we have available. This is for the relationship that is, rather than the one that never was.

And finally, to **"Little Liz"**: We are finally out of the courtroom. The verdict is in: you are free. Now, it's time to build.

CONTENTS

"Before the theology, there was impact."

"Faith is not the denial of trauma; it is what keeps the pieces from scattering."

"Preparation does not produce obedience automatically. I still had to agree."

PREFACE
THE LAW OF
BREADCRUMBS

I have felt, on a very cellular level, that I was made for something significant. I say that without arrogance, because for most of my adult life, I did not know what that something was. I just knew the feeling. I knew the quiet urgency of it. And I kept following it, one small prompt at a time, without a map.

We often spend our lives waiting for a "burning bush" moment—a dramatic, unmistakable sign that we are ready for our purpose. We wait for the extraordinary before we agree to be equipped.

But as I looked back at my life while preparing this manuscript, I realized that God rarely speaks in spectacles. He speaks in **breadcrumbs**. He speaks through a court-ordered job at a Boys and Girls Club, a frustrating afternoon at a Montessori school, and a two-week acceleration into a role I didn't even read the description for. He speaks through twenty years of administrative spreadsheets, school attendance logs, and Standard Operating Procedures (SOPs) that I once thought were just a career—and that turned out to be the bricks and mortar of a divine foundation.

I did not come up with the word "breadcrumbs." As it turns out, my mother did.

In August 2016, Cynthia Elaine Davenport sat down and wrote a letter to her granddaughters, Elise and Madelyn. She was writing about faith, about trust, about the invisible forces that conspire to move us toward our destiny. And in the middle of that letter, she wrote this: that alchemy and serendipity are like breadcrumbs that help lead you toward your destiny, one step at a time.

She wrote that sentence eight years before this book existed. I didn't know until we found it. And when I did, I understood: the title of this book was always hers.

She also had a sign on her refrigerator that I passed every day. It read: "In the end it was good. So if it is not good, it is not the end."

That sign is the theology of this entire book in two sentences. Because every 'bad' season I walked through eventually revealed itself as something else entirely — preparation hiding inside the pause. The key was understanding that they were not detours from the path. They were the path.

Whether you are in a season of floating or a season of sprinting, my prayer is that these chapters help you recognize that nothing—not the detours, not the delays, not the devastated child still living somewhere inside you—is ever wasted. *What is for you is for you.* But you have to be willing to do the work to move when the bell rings. I am no longer hiding behind my mother's skirts or sending the call to voicemail. I am standing in the responsibility of my readiness.

The finish line is in sight. It's time to run.

AUTHOR'S NOTE
ON TRAUMA AND FAITH

The pages you are about to read were written from the intersection of deep-seated trauma and unwavering faith. For many years, I believed these two things could not coexist. If I had faith, I shouldn't feel the "ice" of past hurts, and if I had trauma, my faith must be fractured.

I have learned that the opposite is true. Faith is the tool we use to excavate trauma.

In the months following my mother's death in May 2024, I was having a hard time reconciling the woman she raised me to be with the woman being swallowed by grief. The strong one. The capable one. The one who figured things out. That woman and the one weeping on the floor at two in the morning felt like strangers to each other. Writing this book is what saved my sanity. It is what gave grief somewhere to go that wasn't just inside my body.

Watching my mother decline was like watching the slow snuffing out of a candle. For a long time, I thought I had all the time in the world to enjoy its beauty. Then, little by little, I noticed the dimming. Sometimes it felt like the light was holding steady—and I would exhale. Then it could not be ignored any longer that the end was near. At what seemed like the snap of fingers, that light was extinguished. Gone. And what comes after that kind of gone is not something anyone fully prepares you for.

That's where this book begins.

This is not a religious dissertation or a political argument. It is not a prescription for how you should grieve, how quickly you should heal, or which God you should be calling on when the floor gives out. This is my story, told through my faith, shaped by my losses, and offered without judgment of where you are in yours. I only ask that the "no judgment" be reciprocated. Come as you are. That's the only requirement.

In these pages, I speak openly about **"Little Liz"**—the four-year-old version of myself who was devastated by my parents' divorce. The 'Big Scary Mall' is the most accurate way I know to describe the cellular disorientation of grief — that heart-pounding moment when the hand you were holding is suddenly gone, and the world becomes vast and echoing and unfamiliar.

My mother was a writer. She kept journals. She wrote essays on faith and healing. She wrote a letter to my daughters that she began in 2016 — a letter about trust, about purpose, about alchemy and the mysterious forces that guide us toward our destiny.

It was in that letter that she first used the word "breadcrumbs" to describe the way God leads us, one quiet step at a time. The title of this book was always hers.

In that way, you are not holding one writer's story. You are holding two.

If you are carrying your own ice block—if you feel like a child wandering an endless aisle looking for a hand to hold—know this: **healing is not the absence of the scar. It is the integration of the story.** My hope is that by sharing my process of melting the ice and stepping out of the freeze, you will find the audacity to stand in your own light.

The candle is not the only source of light. Sometimes, when it goes out—that's when we finally discover we were always carrying our own.

— *Elizabeth J. Harris, MSW*

INTRODUCTION FOLLOWING THE BREADCRUMBS

Before the theology, there was impact. Before the vision, there was velocity. Before the thaw, there was collision.

In July 2002, I was sitting in the back passenger seat of a car traveling at highway speed when my world turned upside down. The car struck the median. Metal screamed against concrete. Glass burst outward. Gravity shifted.

There are moments in life that divide time into before and after. This was one of them.

I do not remember the sound of the flip. I do not remember the moment of being thrown. But I remember waking up on hot asphalt after landing. I remember the force of my back against the ground—and the sudden inability to move. I remember the New Mexico sun blazing down on my face that July afternoon; the heat felt relentless, almost indifferent.

I drifted in and out of consciousness. One moment there was sky. The next, fragments of voices. Then nothing. Eventually, I heard the helicopter blades—the sharp rhythm cutting through the air as it ascended. I remember being lifted, the sound of the machinery carrying me toward help. And then darkness again.

I had gotten engaged just the month before. Somewhere between the asphalt and the hospital, between awareness and unconsciousness, one tethering concern surfaced with startling clarity: my engagement ring. I remember asking—maybe a nurse, maybe a doctor—if it was still on my finger.

It seems like a trivial thing to worry about when your life is hanging in the balance, but that ring was more than a piece of gold. It was the physical anchor to the life I had been planning. In that moment of total chaos, I was desperate to know that the trauma I was currently enduring hadn't already erased the future I had been promised. I needed to know that the woman who woke up in that hospital bed would still be the same woman who had a wedding to plan and a life to build with DuJuan.

Fixating on that ring was an act of 'bracing.' It was my way of trying to hold onto a sense of self that felt like it was slipping through my fingers. In the years since that afternoon on the asphalt, I have learned that strength alone merely braces against the world. Bracing is a state of high alert that consumes energy; it keeps you rigid and perpetually prepared for a blow that has already landed. It is a high-functioning suspension—an attempt to stay safe by staying still.

Faith is not the denial of trauma. It is what keeps the pieces from scattering.

For decades, I lived as a woman waiting for a permission slip that had already been signed in the secret places of my soul. I spent twenty years meticulously building Standard Operating Procedures for others, unaware that I was simultaneously being prepared for a mission that required more than just administrative excellence—it required an unthawing of my very existence.

In the pages that follow, I invite you to see something I once struggled to recognize while still walking the path: that every perceived detour was actually a divine appointment. I now understand that God's hand was steadying my breath even when the world went dark, guiding me through that 2002 accident, the quiet decades of professional waiting, and the profound catalyst of my mother's death in 2024. None of these moments were random; they were the "infrastructure of care" being built in the dark. They were the breadcrumbs that led me to reside in Him, proving that my preparation was never a limitation, but a prerequisite for my purpose.

This book is the record of that reporting for duty. It is the evidence that when the safety net of our earthly attachments falls away, the only thing left standing is the truth that we are, and have always been, a divine extension of the Most High.

The Extinguished Flame

Losing my mother was not sudden. It unfolded slowly.

For nearly fifty years, I believed I had endless time with her. Gradually, her physical decline became impossible to ignore. There were stretches when her health seemed steady—moments when we convinced ourselves she might hold on indefinitely. But over time, the changes were undeniable.

She was diagnosed with Lupus and congestive heart failure in 1994. Years later, a stroke forced her to relearn how to read, write, and speak—a devastating adjustment for a woman who loved language and conversation. Within the final decade of her life, she required heart stents, depended on oxygen, and relied on a cane to steady her steps, much to her chagrin. There were flare-ups that left her bedridden; episodes of chest pain that forced her to pause and assess whether it was heartburn—or something more serious.

And yet, she lived fully. She did not look like what she had survived. The oxygen tank, the cane, the stents—they were realities of her body, but never the headline of her identity. She traveled, attended baseball games, and went to live theater. Earlier in life, she had to pivot from dreams of becoming a lawyer to fighting for Social Security disability benefits—a long process that initially ended in denial before finally ending in approval. Resilience was not new to her.

The Decision

In the months leading up to May 2024, her decline accelerated. One night she began vomiting bile. My brother Joe and I panicked; she did not. Calmly, she told us she would not return to the hospital. It was not fear; it was a decision.

Two to three months before her death, she gradually stopped eating. Hospice stepped in. Friends, her sister-in-law, and one of her nieces rotated in and out to sit with her so I could continue working until I was able to take FMLA leave. Being her caregiver was sacred—and exhausting. In that role, time feels fragile. Every routine carries the quiet awareness that it may be the last.

And then came the night we waited.

There were no machines, no hospital monitors, no sterile beeping, and no fluorescent lights. She was home, and that mattered to her. She had been clear for years: she would not die in a hospital or nursing facility. She would remain at home. Hospice delivered an adjustable medical bed, but there were no tubes tethering her to machines. Just oxygen and other supplies should they be needed.

I placed her favorite scented candles around the room and let her playlist play softly from her phone—songs she loved, songs that felt familiar. If she was leaving, I wanted her surrounded by what comforted her. While the hospice bed remained in her bedroom, my husband and I moved her mattress into the next room and placed it on the floor—close enough to hear her breathing, close enough to respond if it changed.

The Final Watch

That final night, her breathing shifted. It had changed before—slower, shallower—but this felt different. I called the hospice nurse. She arrived, examined her gently, and said what nurses say carefully in those moments: "She likely won't survive the night."

There is clarity when someone else names what you already sense. I began making calls to her son and her brother. My aunt, uncle, and cousin arrived near midnight. The house was dim. Candles flickered. Music played softly in the background. My brother was driving from Atlanta, and we knew he would not make it in time. The reality settled quietly over the room.

We gathered around her bed and remembered her out loud. We told stories about her discipline, her humor, and her stubbornness. We repeated her phrases and recalled the way she handled challenges. There is something sacred about remembering someone while they are still physically present. Her breathing continued—slow and uneven— while the candles flickered and we laughed with quiet sincerity.

The Shift in Rhythm

Then I noticed it: a pause. Slightly longer than the others. I leaned in. I had been sleeping near that breath for days; I knew its rhythm. This pause was different. The room was mid-conversation when I leaned in closer and watched her chest.

Nothing. I waited. Nothing.

In that suspended second, I knew. She had slipped away while we were remembering her. Almost as if she chose that moment, thinking: *They're laughing. They're together. They're okay. I can go now.*

"Wait," I said softly. The room stilled. There was no chaos, no alarms, no urgent instructions. Just breath that had been there—and then wasn't. The hospice nurse had prepared us, but preparation does not remove impact.

I felt it in my body first—that tightening. It was the same internal brace I experienced in 2002 when the car flipped. Different moment, same nervous system. Finality has weight. It settled into the room through tears, hands held, and quiet confirmations. But beneath it all, peace remained. She died at home, in soft light, with familiar music, surrounded by love.

The Silence After

Later, after calls were made and paperwork began—after my brother arrived to a house where the breathing had already stopped—I lay back down on the mattress on the floor. The candles had burned low. The playlist had ended. The light of her physical presence was gone. In a single heartbeat, laughter had turned to tears, and beneath the stillness, a question rose: *Now who am I without her?*

The accident in 2002 taught my body how to survive impact; this night taught my heart how to endure it. I moved. I functioned. I braced — because survival was familiar. But beneath the composure, something in me held its own breath. I understood then that endurance and healing are not the same thing. It would take time—and gentleness—to exhale again.

Still Together, Just a Little Different

Grief rearranges the furniture of your soul.

When you walk back into the room of your life after a major loss, nothing sits where it used to. The light comes in at an unfamiliar angle, and even the silence has a different weight to it. When my mother died, the world did not stop spinning; instead, it shifted slightly off its axis. Gravity changed, yet I was expected to keep walking as if the ground were still solid beneath my feet.

People often say that "time heals," but I have found that isn't entirely true. Time alone is passive. It does not heal; it merely reveals what you choose to do with the wound. You can let the wound fester into a permanent "bracing" against life, or you can allow it to be the site of a new, deeper connection.

Suspended Between Two Realities

In the early months of this new season, I lived suspended between two seemingly contradictory realities.

In the first reality, she was gone. Her voice no longer echoed through our home, and her laughter no longer drifted down the hallways. This was the reality of the physical absence, the one the world sees.

But in the second reality, she felt impossibly present. This wasn't just a metaphor or a sentimental feeling; it was a truth I felt on a cellular level. I found myself speaking to her out loud the way I always had: 'Mom, what do you think about this?'

In those moments, the air would remain still, but something inside me would settle, as if the question had been received and the "team" was still in session.

The Theological Scaffolding of Moana

It was during this period of transition that God used a children's movie to provide the theological scaffolding I needed to bridge these two realities.

In Moana, when Gramma Tala passes away, she doesn't vanish — she transitions, remaining a constant presence in a different form. In a moment of deep despair, she finds Moana and offers five words that rearranged something in me: "Still together. Just a little different."

That phrase became the theological bridge I didn't know I needed. It gave me language for what I was experiencing. It was simply a different type of presence. My mother had not left. She had changed form. And accepting that was the first step from survival to building. I will return to this moment more fully in the pages ahead.

The Physical Weight of Grief

I had always thought of grief as something that lived entirely in the mind—a collection of memories, a cycle of tears, or a heavy cloud over one's spirit. I never expected it to be a physical stowaway in my own body. But after my mother slipped away on May 20, 2024, I learned that the heart doesn't just break metaphorically; it can actually hurt as if it's been bruised.

The Sensation of the "Allness"

The physical manifestation of my loss began toward the end of July 2024. It started as a persistent pressure, a literal weight sitting directly on my chest. It felt like I had been punched in the heart area, and the sensation was so intense that I began to fear for my health. With my mother's history of heart disease and my own struggles with hypertension, I couldn't afford to be careless.

I began a carousel of medical appointments, desperate to find a physical cause for the crushing sensation.

But every test came back with the same result: a clean bill of health. My physical heart was fine, yet the pain remained. That was when the realization hit me with the force of a lightning bolt: **this was the weight of the "allness" of my relationship with my mother.**

The Severed Anchor

If you have never experienced a bond like the one my mother and I shared, it is difficult to describe the profound vacancy her absence created. We were more than just mother and daughter; we were a team, each other's constant companion and "person" in almost every sense of the word. For nearly five decades, our lives ran on the same current — she was my mentor, my counselor, my person. And I became hers.

She was my safety net, the one who held up a mirror to my strength when I couldn't see it myself, just as I stood as her advocate through every season of her health journey. We navigated the world together, celebrating each other's triumphs and picking up the pieces whenever the other was hurting. This daily, physical connection was so deeply etched into my very essence that when it was severed, my body had no map for the sudden, heavy stillness. The pain in my chest was the physical outcry of a soul that had lost its first best friend and its most familiar anchor.

The Bridge to 1982

The chest pain was my body's way of screaming what my mind was still trying to grasp: "I didn't know this level of pain existed." This physical trauma also acted as a bridge to my past.

In my journal, I noted that my 46-year-old self was suddenly identifying with the four-year-old girl I once was—the one standing in a courthouse, lost and devastated by her parents' divorce. The pain in my chest was the same "sad, scared, and devastated" feeling I had carried decades ago. It was as if my body had stored that original trauma in a "block of ice" that later solidified into a protective barrier.

To move forward, I realized I couldn't just think my way out of grief. I had to allow the "allness" of my love for my mother to melt that ice, acknowledging that the weight in my chest wasn't a heart attack, but a heart finally allowing itself to feel the full magnitude of a love that remains "still together, just a little different."

I wrote the following words in my journal on May 21, 2025—one year and one day after she died. And somewhere between the grief and the growing, between the bracing and the building, something shifted into place.

From behind my mother's skirts, I must now stand into the fullness of the woman God created me to be.

That is what this book is. Not the end of the story. The beginning of the standing.

PART I

THE FOUNDATION OF IMPACT

> *"Before the theology, there was impact."*

CHAPTER ONE

THE FIRST THEOLOGY

On the woman who showed me what faith looked like.

"I decided that I was going to live until I die!"

— Cynthia Elaine Davenport, The Lupus Book

Before the Theology

Before I understood what faith looked like in practice, I watched it live through my mother.

My mother was not a woman who talked about God from a safe distance. She did not reserve her theology for Sundays or tuck it away for moments of crisis. She wore it like a second skin — through doctor's appointments and Uber rides, through the long years of disability checks and the quiet discipline of affirmations she spoke over herself.

She was the first evidence I ever had that faith was not wishful think-ing. It was a decision. A posture. A practice of choosing life even when the body said otherwise.

She was also, for a good portion of my adult life, my neighbor.

She lived downstairs, in her own apartment, in the 4-family home that my husband and I own. I want you to hold that for a moment, be-cause it is easy to read that as a logistical detail and miss what it actually means. My mother was not a phone call away or a cross-town drive. She was a flight of stairs. I saw her multiple times a day — everyday. She was present for both miscarriages and both pregnancies. She was there for doctor's appointments and grocery runs and the mundane miracle of a shared meal. My daughters, Elise and Madelyn, grew up with their grandmother woven into the fabric of every ordinary day.

And Elise? She was Mommy C's baby. Elise came into the world wearing Cynthia's face. As Elise grew out of her infant and toddler years, she gravitated toward her Mommy C with a particular loyalty. Maddie stayed closer to me. The arrangement settled naturally into something we named out loud with a laugh: "You got one, I got one."

Love made her Mommy C. She had wanted a different name, but the children she adored took the naming in their own direction, and she followed them there, as she always did. Mommy C. Three syllables that carried a whole theology of belonging.

Before I knew the word breadcrumb, before I had language for divine preparation or hidden seasons or the long game of obedience, I had her. She was the first theology.

What She Left Behind

My mother was the kind of woman who does not look like what she had survived. Her doctor would learn this about her early. After her first admittance to the Intensive Care Unit, the doctor reviewed her chart with the grave expression of someone reading a verdict. What he saw on paper was serious — a condition with a prognosis that warranted concern. What he did not expect was her. What he could not have anticipated was the gap between the chart and the woman sitting across from him.

On paper my condition was grave, but in person I was upbeat and positive. I was determined not to allow the diagnosis to define me.

— Cynthia Elaine Davenport, The Lupus Book, Introduction

She was diagnosed with lupus and congestive heart failure in 1994. She was a single mother, who had quit a stable job at Illinois Bell to go back to school. Her ultimate goal was to become a lawyer. Then her body delivered a different verdict.

The lupus redirected her dream. And then it settled in for a thirty-year conversation with her spirit, a conversation she refused to let her body win.

For thirty years, she navigated that diagnosis with a stubbornness the disease could not match. She continued to build a life — traveling, attending baseball games, going to live theater. She fought for Social Security disability benefits through a long process that eventually ended in approval. She began writing her own manuscript about what it meant to survive with lupus, working out on the page the mind-body-spirit theology she had not just theorized but lived. She wrote about the breadcrumbs. She coined the very metaphor that became the title of mine. In her later years, when her body required a cane and eventually oxygen, she adapted. She kept going.

She also, somehow, remained consistently upbeat and positive.

I watched her navigate the bureaucracy of Medicaid with a dignity that should not have been required of her. I was there for the hospital visits and the hospice planning. And in all of it, there was a consistent, daily refusal to be defined by the difficulty of her circumstances. She was making a disciplined decision, every single day, about what she would allow to be the headline of her identity.

"I decided that I was going to live until I die!"

That was her declaration. She wrote it down. She meant it absolutely.

Five Things She Taught Me

Some lessons arrive fully formed. Others take decades to recognize as lessons at all.

I spent over four decades watching my mother, and it was only after she was gone — only in the particular silence that follows losing the person who was the mirror you did not know you were looking into — that I could finally see the curriculum she had been teaching me all along.

1. Build your financial future while you can.

My mother was brilliant and tenacious. She worked hard, made sacrifices, and did the best she could with what she had. And she would be the first to tell you that the financial piece came late. The lupus had derailed the career she planned. The disability check was not enough. She spent the last decade of her life doing the slow, hard work of trying to change her relationship with money. She made real progress. She simply did not have the time she needed to finish what she started.

She used to say that she wished she had been more financially literate earlier. Not in those exact words, but the sentiment was unmistakable. She had a plan for her career. She did not have a plan B when that career was overturned. And watching her navigate her final years — the limited medical options, the weight of a generation trying to catch up — I made a quiet, fierce promise: I would do this differently. She gave me everything she had — and then she gave me something more: her example, and the time to learn from it while I still could.

2. Don't die alone, broke, and with no legacy.

She was rich in spirit, rich in love, rich in theological depth I am still unpacking. But the material resources were thin, and watching her navigate her final years was not always easy. I do not want my daughters to carry that weight. I do not want them navigating the logistics of loss while simultaneously trying to grieve. That is what she could not protect me from — and it is part of the reason Cynthy's Kids, Inc. exists.

3. **Chase your dreams, even when life throws a curveball.**

   She walked away from stability because the dream of becoming a lawyer was louder than the comfort of the familiar. Then the lupus arrived, and the dream changed shape. She did not become a lawyer. But she became something else: a writer, a theologian, a woman who studied the laws of the spirit with the same rigor she would have brought to a courtroom. She became, among other things, the woman who wrote the word that is now the foundation of this book.

   The dream redirected. It did not disappear. That distinction matters more than I can fully say.

4. **Love always wins.**

   I am still learning this one. My mother modeled it in a thousand different ways — the way she advocated for me without bitterness when it would have been easier to let me fight alone, the way she met her own heartbreaks with a gentleness I am still trying to inherit. She demonstrated, consistently, that love was not a feeling you waited for but a decision you made, over and over, in the direction of the people entrusted to your care. I will come back to this thread throughout this book, because it runs beneath every other lesson she left me. It is the reason I can speak about forgiveness without resentment. It is the reason any of this exists at all.

5. **Love yourself first.**

   She did this imperfectly, as all of us do. But she pointed the way. She showed me that you cannot sustain what you are not willing to replenish. She showed me what it looked like to put the oxygen mask on first — stewardship before selflessness. Her affirmations were maintenance. They were her way of keeping the internal architecture stable enough to hold up everything she was responsible for holding. I am still learning to do this without guilt. She gave me the template and I am still following it.

Three Memories I Keep

There is a specific quality to the memories that surface after you lose someone. They are not always the grand occasions. Sometimes they are the small, ordinary moments that carry, in retrospect, the whole weight of what you shared.

These are three of mine.

The Airport.

When I was a kid, my mother would occasionally send me to California for a few weeks in the summer, to visit family. I was young enough that traveling alone required the accompaniment of flight attendants, the careful handoff between gate and gate.

On one of those trips home, my mother was late.

I remember being one of the last children left in the terminal, sitting with the flight attendants, the crowds thinning around me. And then — I saw her. Running. Arms already open before she had reached me. I let go of the flight attendant's hand and started running too. Both of us moving at full speed toward each other, arms outstretched, the way it happens in movies except this was real and this was my mother and when we reached each other it was everything.

The flight attendant caught up and said, with a smile: "Well, I guess you must be mom."

I have held that image for decades. The running. The outstretched arms. The way she came for me the moment she could. I did not know it then, but that scene is the whole book. She always came running. She always had her arms out. Even when she was late — she always came.

The Wine and the Record Player.

My mother did my makeup for prom. That in itself is a memory worth keeping — the gentleness of it, the way she gave me that rite of passage with her own hands. But the memory I carry most from that season is what happened after.

While I was out with my friends, my mother went to a bar with some of her own people and celebrated. Her child was graduating. A chapter was closing. She was going to mark it her way. By the time she got home, she was joyfully, unapologetically in the spirit of the evening.

And then — and this is the part I treasure most — she decided she wanted to share that joy with me. Right before I left for college, she got us a couple of bottles of wine, put on the record player, and we sat in that apartment together, the two of us, and we laughed. She wanted me to experience what it felt like, she said, while I was still somewhere safe. She wanted to be the context for that particular lesson.

I will not tell you it was my first time. She did not know that. What I will tell you is that it was one of the most alive evenings of my life — the two of us on either side of some invisible threshold between her adulthood and my own, laughing our way across it together. The record player spinning. The wine poured. My mother deciding that even in this, she could be present for me.

That was her. All the way down.

The Springfield Trip.

The year Barack Obama named Joe Biden as his running mate, my mother decided we were going to witness it.

She got us up before sunrise and drove to Springfield, Illinois. We were among the first people to arrive and stood at the front of the crowd in a summer heat that rose around us with an intensity that tested every person in that crowd. I thought we might pass out. Fortunately, we did not.

We shook hands with the candidates and their wives. I took pictures and made her a Shutterfly book from those photographs. She displayed it in her living room for the rest of her life.

What I remember most is not the history of it, though I understood I was standing inside a moment that would be recorded and retold. What I remember most is her face. The particular quality of her joy on that day. The way she stood in that crowd with a complete ownership of the moment — as if bearing witness to something important was exactly the kind of thing a woman like her was supposed to do.

She was right. It was.

The Permission She Gave Without Knowing

There is a moment I return to often. One that only became fully legible to me when I was raising my own daughters and faced with the particular weight of being a mother who wants to do right by her children without crushing them in the process.

I was in college, taking a statistics course that was beating me. I had always been a student who did well — academics were the baseline, the expectation I had absorbed and made my own. The thought of getting a C felt like a specific kind of failure: the kind that would disappoint my mother.

I told her what was happening. I braced for the response.

She looked at me and asked: "Did you do your best?"

I said yes.

"That's all I can ask of you," she said. "When you've done your best and given your all, I can respect your effort. There is such a thing as a hard C."

My father had a similar and fitting saying that summarized the same sentiment. "When all you can do is all you can do. That's all you can do." It's simple, but absolutely unforgettable. I stood there recalibrating.

In a single exchange, she handed me back something I did not realize I had been carrying: the anxiety of needing to exceed in order to be enough. She gave me permission to release it. She told me that effort was the currency that mattered, not the grade on the transcript.

I got the hard C. I carried her answer with me for twenty more years.

When my daughter Elise began struggling in one of her more demanding courses, I heard my mother's voice. I asked the question she had asked me. I watched my daughter's shoulders drop slightly, the way mine must have dropped. The permission traveling forward, one more generation.

That is what I mean when I say my mother was the first theology. She would be the first to laugh at her being described as 'perfect'. The things she understood and practiced became the instruction manual I reached for in every season that followed. She was not only modeling faith for me. She was transmitting it.

Her Own Words

I want to close this chapter the way I am learning to close everything: by getting out of the way.

My mother was a writer. She wrote essays. She wrote reflections. She began writing a manuscript about what it meant to live with lupus — about the mind-body-spirit connection she had not just theorized but tested across decades of daily practice. She wrote about the breadcrumbs. About the thaw. About the sacred indwelling. She wrote it all down before I wrote a word of this manuscript.

She was a co-author before the book existed.

In one of those documents she wrote this:

I always look for and expect good to flow to me. This is a powerful declaration. The word "I" professes my personal investment in this affirmation; "always" means that I unequivocally set my intention toward the words that follow. "Look for and expect" is pregnant with optimism and anticipation.

I co-create those dreams with God. It's a divine relationship — a sacred covenant. I use my energy to attract the experiences I want to manifest and God moves on my behalf to create those experiences. In this way, the good that I expect flows easily to me.

— Cynthia Elaine Davenport, "I Always Look for and Expect Good to Flow to Me" (April 10, 2017)

Seven years before she died — the lupus still making its thirty-year argument with her body — she wrote that and meant every word.

That is the woman who raised me. That is the woman whose face lives in my daughter's face, whose voice I still hear when I need to remember what courage sounds like without performance, what faith looks like when it is not dressed up for Sunday.

She decided she was going to live until she died.

And she did — completely, fully, beautifully, on her own terms — until the last breath.

The theology was always hers first.

I am just learning to walk in it.

25

Who was your first theologian — the person who modeled faith for you before you had language for it? What did they teach you without ever calling it a lesson?

____

____

____

____

____

____

____

____

____

____

CHAPTER TWO

THE COURTHOUSE ECHO

*On the wound that travels — and the
child who was never meant to carry it.*

∞ —— ∞

"I've been expected to act as an adult since I was a child."

— Elizabeth J. Harris, MSW, February 2025

She was four years old.

She did not know the word *divorce*. She did not know what a judge was, or why this particular stranger in black robes had the power to decide her life. She knew only that the room was too big, that the ceilings were too high, and that the adults around her were doing the thing adults do when something is falling apart: they were being very, very quiet.

She knew that she was being asked a question.

She knew that the question was about which parent she wanted to live with.

She did not know how to answer it. She did not know that she was not supposed to have to.

The Beginning of the Brace

That little girl was me. And that moment — a four-year-old standing in a Chicago courthouse in 1982, trying to make a choice that no child should be required to make — became the origin wound I would carry without fully knowing it for the next four decades.

I walked out of that courthouse and did what children do when the adults around them don't know what else to ask for: I complied. I answered. I stood still in a room full of legal language I could not parse, and I held myself together because the situation seemed to require it.

That was my very first act of bracing.

I didn't have a name for it then. I didn't know that the stillness I was perfecting in that courthouse would become the template for how I handled every hard thing that followed. I just knew that the world had suddenly gotten very loud and very big, and that standing still and staying quiet was how you survived it.

What that four-year-old could not have understood at the time: none of it was her fault.

The little girl in the courthouse did not cause her parents' marriage to end. She was not the reason the family divided. She was not too much, or not enough, or the wrong kind of child. She was simply a child in a circumstance that was too large for her, being asked to navigate a world designed for adults.

She was not responsible for the divorce. She was only responsible for surviving it.

And survive it she did. The way children always do: by becoming very, very good at being okay.

Little Liz and the Big Scary Mall

Do you remember what it felt like to lose a hand in a crowd? One moment it was there, and then it wasn't — and the world became enormous and terrifying all at once.

One moment the world is navigable — you have an anchor, a direction, a sense of where you belong. The next moment, the hand is gone, and the world becomes vast and echoing and entirely too large. Your heart pounds. The crowd shifts. Every adult face you see is a stranger's face. And you cannot make sense of what just happened or why, only that you are on the wrong side of it.

That is what I call the Big Scary Mall — the specific terror of separation, the safety net dropping without warning, and the way your entire nervous system rewrites its instructions in response.

The little girl in the courthouse experienced the Big Scary Mall. The hand she had been holding — the hand of an intact family, of a world in which both parents lived under one roof and the future was predictable — was gone. And no one in that room had a map for where she was supposed to go next.

So, she made one.

She learned to read the room. She learned to stay quiet when quiet was required. She learned that strength meant not falling apart, that love meant not adding to the weight already in the room, and that the safest version of herself was the composed one. She became — as so many children in the middle of adult crises become — very skilled at not needing things.

I have called her Little Liz ever since the day I finally had a name for what I was carrying.

She has been with me every step of the way.

What the Courthouse Left Empty

The courthouse created a vacancy — deep, cellular, invisible to everyone around me. The hand that should have been holding mine was gone. And for the next four decades, I quietly rebuilt that sense of anchor wherever I could.

My mother became that anchor. Fully and completely.

I did not understand the full weight of this until the night before she died, when I sat with a journal and a pen and wrote it out plainly, almost involuntarily. Every question led to the same answer. Hard seasons — my momma. New motherhood — my momma. Financial uncertainty, spiritual grounding, the person who saw my strength when I couldn't see it myself — my momma. Every single one.

Reading it back, I saw what the list was actually saying. It was not just a tribute. It was a map of everything the courthouse had emptied out — and everything my mother had quietly, faithfully, persistently refilled. She had been the safety net. The orienting hand. The voice that said, *"You can do this."* She had been, in ways I could not have articulated at four years old, the answer to the question the courthouse left unanswered.

And now I was going to have to learn to navigate without her.

The Big Scary Mall was back. And this time, the hand I reached for wasn't there to take.

Expected to Act as an Adult

There is something else the courthouse did that I have only recently found language for.

It required me to perform adulthood at four years old.

In February 2025, while working through this manuscript and sitting with what Little Liz had actually carried, I wrote this in my journal: *"I've been expected to act as an adult since I was a child."*

A courthouse appearance requires composure. It requires listening and responding and communicating a preference in adult language. It requires a child to suspend childhood and perform a kind of competence she has not yet grown into. And no one in that room — not the lawyers, not the judge, not the parents — had stopped to ask whether any of this was appropriate. It was simply expected.

That expectation did not end when we left the courthouse.

For years, bracing — that pattern of managing and composing and holding myself together before anyone could see me come apart — was how I moved through the world. It looked like competence. It looked like strength. But beneath it was a four-year-old who had learned that her feelings were less important than the correct answer. That being okay was a performance she owed the room.

The wounds we leave unaddressed become the architecture of our limitations.

That is what the courthouse built without my consent. It built a woman who was very good at being okay, and very unpracticed at asking for what she needed.

What Unhealed Things Carry

I have learned that origin wounds do not stay put.

You can put decades between yourself and the courthouse. You can build a life that looks nothing like the life of that four-year-old. You can become a professional, a wife, a mother, a woman of faith — a woman people call *strong* and mean it sincerely. And still, if you have not gone back for the child you left in that room, she will find a way to make herself known.

For me, she made herself known in May 2024, when my mother died.

I was 46 years old. And in the weeks that followed the loss, I felt it. It was old grief wearing new grief's clothes — the same cellular language the four-year-old and the forty-six-year-old suddenly spoke together: sad, scared, and devastated.

In my journal, I wrote it plainly: *My 46-year-old self is now identifying with the loss of my 4-year-old self. They may be different types of losses, but the effects hit me with the same emotions. Sad, scared, and devastated.*

The hand was gone again. The Big Scary Mall was back.

And I finally understood that I had never really left it.

The Bridge Between 1982 and 2024

Grief has a way of becoming an excavation if you let it. And what I found when the grief of 2024 broke me open was the 1982 wound still waiting at the bottom — perfectly preserved, sealed in ice.

When you are a child and the world splits in two, you cannot process all of it at the time. Your nervous system is not built for it; your vocabulary is not equal to it; the adults around you are too consumed with their own grief to hold space for yours. So, you hold it yourself, the only way a child knows how: by storing it in the body. By tightening the shoulders. By learning to breathe shallowly. By becoming very still in rooms that feel too large.

That stored grief becomes the ice block. And it waits.

I thought the loss of my mother was singular. I did not understand, until I was sitting inside it, that what I was grieving was everything at once: the mother I had just lost, and the mother I had needed at four years old in a courthouse. The family that had been whole and then wasn't. The child who had been asked to choose and had never been told, clearly and simply, that the choosing was not hers to carry.

This is what unhealed things do. They wait for a crack in the composure — and then they come through all at once.

The grief of 2024 was the crack. And Little Liz came through it with everything she had been holding.

What She Was Waiting to Hear

I have thought a great deal about what Little Liz needed in that courthouse, and what she still needed forty-two years later.

She needed to know that the divorce was not her fault.

She needed to know that the right answer to "which parent do you want to live with?" was: *I am four years old. I should not have to answer this question.* She needed someone in that room to understand that placing that choice in a child's hands places a weight there that the child was never designed to carry.

She needed to know that the Big Scary Mall had an exit — that the hand she lost was not the last hand that would reach for hers.

She needed, eventually, to meet the woman she would become.

That woman — this woman — has spent years learning to go back for her. To say the things that needed to be said, even if they are forty-two years late. To pick up the child in the courthouse and tell her:

"You were not responsible for what broke. You were only responsible for surviving it. And you did. And we are still here."

This is the quiet work. Going back for the child you left behind and giving her what she needed before you can build what you're called to build.

I've learned that you cannot lead from the courthouse. You cannot build a legacy while a four-year-old is still bracing in the corner of your nervous system. Again, the wounds we leave unaddressed become the architecture of our limitations. They shape what we reach for and what we refuse. They define the space we allow ourselves to occupy.

Little Liz was not meant to live there forever. The courthouse is not home. It never was.

This book is, in part, the story of getting her out.

What the Bracing Built

The origin wound was instruction as much as it was injury.

The girl who learned to stand still and hold herself together in that courthouse learned something true: that composure is possible, even when the world feels impossible. That you can survive a room that was not designed for you. That the hand you were holding is not the only hand in the world.

She learned it the hard way. She learned it too young. And some of what she learned, I have had to unlearn.

But the foundation of resilience she laid in that courthouse — the quiet insistence that survival was possible, the stubborn refusal to be entirely unmade by what was breaking around her — that was not wrong. It was a first theology, built from the ground up by a four-year-old who had no other tools.

God did not waste the courthouse.

He used it, as He uses all things, as formation. The bracing that began there would eventually need to give way to building — but first, it held. And there were seasons of my life when holding was the only assignment I had.

Bracing kept me alive. The work of this book is about what comes after alive.

Where does your Little Liz still live? What room did she learn to stand still in, and what did she decide about herself in that room — that is still shaping how much space you allow yourself today?

Take a moment. Write her name, or her age, or just the room. And then write one thing she needed to hear that no one said.

She is still waiting. And it is not too late.

____

____

____

____

____

____

____

____

A WORD TO LITTLE LIZ

The chapter opened with a four-year-old standing in a courthouse, making herself small because the room required it of her.

It closes with what I know now — what I recorded on January 31, 2026, the words that came out of me not as craft but as conviction:

"Just because you may be small in frame does not mean that you're not mighty in spirit and in heart and in deed. You are worthy to demand the respect of a room by walking in it, and never let anyone try to tell you different. And if they do try, you hold your head high and your back straight and walk in confidence as you walk around them. And if they won't move out of your way, then you step over them!"

Little Liz, this is for you.

You always deserved to be there.

CHAPTER THREE

THE ICE BLOCK

*On what the body stores when the mind
has learned to forget.*

> *"My body eavesdrops on my mind and it
> responds as directed."*
>
> — Cynthia Elaine Davenport, The Lupus Book

On the first day of January 2026, I went to a chiropractic appointment and came home a different woman. A chiropractor's hands on my spine, a particular spot in my back that had never cooperated, and four words that changed everything.

Dr. Pam had been working with me for months, learning the language of my body the way a skilled interpreter learns a dialect — carefully, patiently, reading what the body says when words fail it. She is one of those rare practitioners who understands that the physical and the spiritual are not as separate as we pretend. She doesn't just treat what hurts. She asks what the hurt has been holding.

That day, she worked her way down my spine, unwinding my neck and shoulders, and when she reached a particular area — what I have come to call *the Area* — the muscles seized. *Immediately.* Like a door slamming on a room that hadn't been opened in years.

She tried again. Same response.

She looked at me and said: *"It's a block of ice."*

I don't know why those five words hit me as hard as they did. I had been managing that spot in my back since at least 2002, when a car accident threw me from a vehicle and placed me on the hot asphalt of a New Mexico highway. I had received treatment, done the work, learned to brace around it. I was managing.

But managing is not the same as healing. And I had been managing for twenty-four years.

When Dr. Pam named it, something unlocked in my understanding. The ice block was the body's record of everything that had never fully been processed — the car accident, yes, but also everything before it and after it. The courthouse in 1982. The accumulated seasons of bracing, of holding still in rooms that felt too large, of absorbing impact and quietly filing it away. The body keeps what the mind moves past. I had moved past a great many things. My back had kept every single one of them.

My mother knew this truth before I had a name for it.

She was quietly writing a book of her own — about living with lupus, about what it meant to inhabit a body that had stopped doing whatever she asked of it. In it she wrote: *"I had to rely on my body to tell me when to stop. But by the time I knew I was in trouble, often it was too late."*

She was writing about lupus. About learning, over the years, to listen before the crisis rather than after it. But reading her words now, I hear something far wider than a diagnosis. I hear a woman describing what it means to live in a body that keeps its own record — a body that knows when the load is too heavy, even when the mind has decided to press on.

She also wrote this: *"My body eavesdrops on my mind and it responds as directed."* She believed the body could be redirected by what the mind chose to believe, chose to feed, chose to speak over itself. She had disciplined her thoughts toward healing. And her body, she said, followed.

Mother and daughter. She discovered this truth through a lupus diagnosis. I discovered it through a block of ice in my spine. Neither of us copied the other. We arrived at the same truth by different bodies — and that means it was always there, waiting in the lineage.

The Resistance Line

I track stocks as part of my own journey toward financial freedom, so when I was sitting with what Dr. Pam had shown me — the ice block, the resistance, the body's stubborn refusal to let that area be touched — I thought immediately of what traders call the resistance line.

Every stock has a ceiling it bounces against. Sometimes it bounces against that ceiling over and over — not rising through, not falling through, just hitting the same point again and again. The market watches. If the stock bounces long enough and then *breaks through* that resistance line, what follows is often a bullish run — new highs, forward momentum, the kind of breakthrough that justified all the waiting.

But you don't want it to fall *through* the resistance line. Because then the ceiling becomes the floor, and the recovery takes much longer.

I had been hitting my resistance line for years. I could feel it — in my body, in my creative life, in the constant sensation of ideas and energy that would build and build and then somehow stall before they could be fully executed. I wasn't lazy — I work seven days a week. Effort was never the problem. But I kept hitting the same ceiling, bouncing off, not breaking through.

Dr. Pam showed me where the resistance line lived. It lived in *the Area.* In the ice block. In the body's record of every hard thing I had walked through and never fully released.

The question she placed before me — without ever saying it aloud — was the same question every serious investor eventually has to face: *Are you going to do the work to break through, or are you going to keep bouncing off the same ceiling for the rest of your life?*

I chose the work.

What God Grows in Frozen Ground

God does not wait for the thaw to begin working. He plants seeds in frozen ground. He sets divine appointments in the middle of seasons that feel like nothing but waiting. He puts the right people in your path before you know you will need them, orchestrates the job that looks like a detour toward the destination you were always heading, and hides blessings inside the consequences of your worst decisions.

I did not know any of this in my twenties or thirties. I was simply moving through seasons, following the quiet promptings, not yet seeing the pattern. But looking back now — with the hindsight of a woman who has finally named her ice block and decided to face it — I can see that the stepping stones were always there. Three moments in particular, each of which I either resented at the time or never fully understood, were the precise places God was working while I was frozen.

The First Stepping Stone: The Boys and Girls Club

I will not dress this up: I made a choice during my college years that I am not proud of. A serious choice with serious consequences. The kind that lands in legal territory, carries a sentence, and leaves a mark on how you see yourself for years afterward.

The consequence was community service. The location assigned was a local Boys and Girls Club.

The mistake was mine. You cannot build what you are called to build while your hand is pointed at someone else for the conditions of your own life. That lesson did not come easily. But it begins here, in a Boys and Girls Club, with court-ordered hours I was deeply ashamed of.

That record was eventually expunged. The legal document was cleared. But for years afterward — including every time I filled out a job application, right up to the position I hold today — I still felt it. That tight, anticipatory dread that the past would surface and undo whatever standing I had worked to build. I still measured my words in certain rooms. Still held my breath in certain conversations. The paper said *expunged*. My body had not gotten the memo.

The legal system closed the file; my nervous system kept a copy. And it will keep that copy until the work of the thaw — real, intentional, unhurried work — reaches that particular shelf.

I walked through those doors with my head down. I felt the weight of that mistake every single time I crossed the threshold. I was embarrassed, and I was certain that everyone could see exactly how I had gotten there.

What I did not know was that God was not watching my entrance. He was already watching my future.

The organization saw something in me that my shame was working overtime to conceal. They hired me as a summer counselor for the next two years. That Boys and Girls Club became the first classroom where I discovered what I was actually built for: working with young people, holding structure high enough that the kids understood they were being held, not just managed.

Near the end of that first summer, I had loosened up on the rules as we built relationship. One of my campers noticed, walked up to me, and asked with genuine concern: *"Ms. Liz, you don't love us anymore?"*

That question never left me. It taught me something I would carry into every school building, every administrative role, every vision for Cynthy's Kids: discipline is not the opposite of love. It is one of love's clearest expressions. Children don't just tolerate structure from someone who cares about them. Eventually, they come to rely on it as a signal that they are safe.

That lesson came from a mistake. God used the consequence of my own poor judgment to plant one of the most important seeds of my eventual calling.

But there is one more thing. Because a coworker from that same job — the job I only had because of a mistake — invited me to a party during Thanksgiving weekend in 1999. That was the night I met my husband, DuJuan.

Nothing — not one moment of it — was wasted.

I did not earn the grace of that meeting. I was not supposed to be there. But God looked at the rubble of my choices and said: *I can work with this.* And He did.

The Second Stepping Stone: Terror Town

When I was sixteen, my mother and her second husband moved us out of the only neighborhood I had ever known. It was abrupt, and it was summer, which meant no proper goodbye to the childhood friendships I had built over a decade. I was, in the vocabulary of a sixteen-year-old, *mad as hell.*

For years afterward, I used that move as a weapon. It was my Ace card in arguments with my mother — the grievance I could deploy whenever I needed to inflict some hurt in return for hurt I was feeling. I am not proud of that. I weaponized the resentment, and I kept it sharp far longer than I should have. That, too, is mine to own.

God, as it turned out, was already seeing around corners I didn't even know were there.

Because we moved to that neighborhood — the one the community knew as Terror Town — I attended Hyde Park Career Academy for my final two years of high school. At Hyde Park, I met a college recruiter from Augustana College. At Augustana, I unexpectedly reconnected with my best friend from sixth grade. She became my college roommate for our freshmen year. She is today the Godmother of both of my daughters.

At Augustana, I also met the woman who is the other great sister-friendship of my adult life. Her only child is my Godchild.

The two women who have stood with me through every season — through grief and growth and the hard, holy work of becoming — exist in my life because my mother moved us to Terror Town. I held that move in my hands like a wound for years. God had already turned it into a gift. I just couldn't see it yet.

The Third Stepping Stone: The FGC Tribe

When I began my role at the Fifth Grade Center, I believed I understood my assignment. Admissions. Attendance. Front office management. I was there to serve the school.

What I did not know — what I could not have known, and what still moves me when I sit with it — is that God had placed me there *for me*. Not just for the school. For me.

He knew what was coming. He knew that in May 2024, my mother would take her final breath. He knew that the woman who had spent forty-six years with Cynthia Davenport as her primary safety net would need somewhere to land when that net was gone. And so — years before I knew I would need it — He built the landing.

The Fifth Grade Center gave me a tribe. Deep, unhurried, meaningful friendships formed in the steady rhythm of shared daily work. These were not surface-level colleagues. They were colleagues who would show up in the worst season of my life and do the kind of showing up that cannot be manufactured.

When my mother passed, they did not send flowers and then wait for me to resume normal operations. They *embraced* me. They held me. They prayed with me when I did not have the words to pray for myself.

God's timing is not accidental. He does not place the support after the need; He places it before — in the form of relationships that look, at the time, like ordinary providence. What looked like colleagues was actually a fortress being assembled, years before I would need to take shelter in it.

The Gatekeeper of the Garden

Much of my professional formation was forged during my time at City Garden Montessori School. If the courthouse in 1982 was the place where I first felt invisible, City Garden was the place where I became most seen.

As the Admissions Coordinator and School Secretary, I was the face of the school — but face meant something specific in that context. It meant the first voice, the first welcome, the one who knew every child's name and every parent's concern. The school's public identity — its mission in the community, its name in the city — that belonged to the executive director and the principal. I was present within the walls. My name was not yet on anything beyond them. And I think, looking back, that the contained nature of that visibility was part of what made it feel safe. I could show up fully — and I did — without yet being asked to stand in front of something and say: this is mine. I built this. Follow me.

Little Liz — the four-year-old who lost her bearings in the Big Scary Mall, who learned to stand still in echoing rooms and wait for a hand that might not come — had spent her life looking for the Information Desk.

At City Garden, *I was the Information Desk.*

I was the one who looked up when the door opened. I was the one who said: *I see you. You are in the right place.* I was providing, for every family that walked through those doors, the exact safety net that Little Liz had once lost. I wasn't just handling admissions, attendance, and front office management at the Fifth Grade Center (FGC) and City Garden Montessori School; I was, without fully knowing it, healing something.

God does not waste formation. City Garden was an apprenticeship — a blueprint in progress that I would eventually recognize as Cynthy's Kids, Inc. I didn't have the name yet. I was just showing up, one faithful day of ordinary labor at a time.

The Thaw Begins

On January 1, 2026, I drove home from Dr. Pam's office with something I had not driven home with before: the name of the thing.

The ice block is real. It is physical — a genuine area of restriction in my spine that has been lodged there since the 2002 accident, waiting with the patience of something that has nothing but time for me to be ready to address it. It is emotional — the accumulated weight of every hard season I walked through by managing rather than healing. And it is spiritual — the gap between the woman I have been carefully maintaining and the woman I am called to become.

I wrote in my journal that night: *Before I can move forward on all of the irons I currently have in the fire, I have to learn how to melt this block of ice in my back and release whatever this blockage is. This has now become a priority.*

Naming it was not the same as releasing it. But it was the beginning of the release. You cannot address what you have not faced. You cannot thaw what you have not agreed to unfreeze.

The stepping stones I have told you about in this chapter — the Boys and Girls Club, Terror Town, the FGC tribe, the City Garden seasons — were not wasted. They were God working in frozen ground, planting what would eventually grow when the warmth arrived.

The warmth is arriving. Slowly, yes. Imperfectly, yes. But arriving.

I have a chiropractor who calls it a block of ice. I have a God who calls it preparation. And I have a woman in the mirror who has finally decided to call it neither a life sentence nor a coincidence — but a thing that is being addressed so that the woman on the other side of the thaw can do the work she was always made to do.

The breadcrumbs were here all along. I was just frozen.

Where is the ice block in your body? Not metaphorically first — literally. Where do you carry tension that has no obvious source, resistance that does not respond to logic, a place that seizes when something gets too close?

Now go one layer deeper: what did you walk through that you managed rather than healed? What mistake did you absorb and move past without ever truly forgiving yourself for it? What record did the official paperwork clear — but your body kept?

You do not have to have it all resolved to begin. You only have to give it a name.

Name it. That is the first thaw.

____

____

____

____

____

____

PART II

THE CATALYST AND THE CALL

"Faith is not the denial of trauma; it is what keeps the pieces from scattering."

CHAPTER FOUR

THE BREATH STOPS

*On love as a physical experience — and
what grief asks of the body that carries it.*

"Home is my haven. It is filled with love and warmth."

— Cynthia Elaine Davenport, The Lupus Book

Let me tell you who my mother was to me before I tell you how I lost her.

When things fell apart with someone I loved — my momma. When I became a mother myself and had no idea what I was doing — my momma. When I found myself behind the eight ball financially — my momma. When I needed someone who could hold the truth of who I was and love me anyway — my momma. When I needed spiritual grounding, a sounding board, a salve for my soul — my momma.

She was more than a support system. She was the *foundation*. And foundations, by design, are the things you never see — until they're gone.

She lived downstairs. Every day, multiple times a day, her presence was woven into the ordinary fabric of my life in a way that only becomes visible in retrospect. She wrote in her Lupus Book: "Home is my haven. It is filled with love and warmth." That was how she lived — and that was how I knew her. I did not know how to imagine a world without her in it. So, I didn't. Right up until the moment the world became that.

The Final Season

She began choosing not to eat in the early months of 2024.

The way a fire goes down when you stop adding wood — slowly, then all at once. She had lived with lupus and congestive heart failure for thirty years, far longer than most people survive such a diagnosis. She had prevailed — graduating college while her doctors were still marveling that she'd survived the hospitalization that started it all. She had decided, early and emphatically, "I am going to live until I die!"

But by spring 2024, she had made her choice. Not eating was her way of deciding, in her quiet and sovereign way, how this final chapter would be written. She used to tell me — sometimes joking, never actually joking — *"You betta not put me in no home!"* She didn't want to die in a hospital room. She didn't want to feel like a burden. She wanted to die the way she had lived: on her own terms, in her own space, surrounded by people who loved her.

So that is what we arranged.

What the phrase *peaceful passing* does not capture is the full weight of what it takes to give someone that gift. There were phone calls to make that no amount of faith can prepare you for. There were fights

— my voice raised, at work, fighting for her hospice access through Medicaid and Medicare while still managing a full-time job. There were calculations running in the back of my mind at all hours: medications, schedules, who could come and sit with her so I didn't have to leave her alone, what I would do about the bills.

Her good friend came. Her sister-in-law. Her niece. We built a rotating schedule out of love and logistics — the way families do when the thing happening is too large for any one person to carry. I eventually took FMLA. By then I had used most of my sick days on her doctor's appointments and on the days when I simply could not be anywhere else. The unpaid stretch was hard. God was not absent from it.

On the morning of Saturday, May 18th, at 5:50 a.m., I called the 24-hour hospice line because she had been moaning and restless for hours. The nurse walked me through the morphine dose. I gave it to her. She settled. She started again. I called back. This was the rhythm of those days — watching, listening, administering, calling, waiting, watching again.

Nurse Kim came to re-evaluate her that morning. She told me something I have never forgotten: *patients end their life much like how they lived it.* If they were stubborn and unconventional, that is how they will usually go. She said she was surprised my mother had lived this long without eating, and she figured it was her personality — and maybe the Pedialyte — that had kept her here longer than expected.

Stubborn and unconventional. I laughed through my exhaustion when she said it. My mother would have been delighted by that assessment.

Sometime during the last days of her life, DuJuan had to sit me down after a hard moment between my mother and me. I had lost my patience — she was not herself, and had done something that risked her safety. I reacted before I could stop myself. He was gentle with me. He said: the person she used to be is in the past. That's not where we are right now. Expecting her words and actions to make sense will only make this harder for both of you. He said my two key words for this whole season needed to be *patience* and *grace*. Patience with her. Grace for myself.

I had needed to hear it. After more tears fell, I eventually went back downstairs and just held her hand.

12:54 a.m.

On the night of May 19th, DuJuan and I were sleeping on her mattress on the floor of her living room. We had been doing that for the last two nights of her life — lying there, not really sleeping, listening to her breathing.

At 12:41 a.m. we called the hospice line again. She was still restless. Nurse Jenn said to give her morphine and lorazepam together. It settled her some. The morning brought more of the same: rattling in the chest, labored breathing, medication adjustments, the hospice nurse conferring with the doctor by phone. By afternoon the morphine dosage had been increased. By evening she was still working too hard to breathe.

Around 10 p.m. Nurse Kim called me back. She said to give her more morphine — and she was on her way. When she arrived and assessed my mother, she said the words I had been dreading and needing at the same time: *she is actively transitioning and will likely not survive the night.*

She did not want to go all the way home because she knew the call to return would come soon.

Her actual words were: *she is as comfortable as she can be, and she will transition peacefully, and likely soon.*

I had already called my brother Joe to tell him he needed to leave now, not in the morning. DuJuan reached Uncle Teddy and Auntie Nette.

While we waited for them to arrive, I pulled a chair to her bedside. I sat with her. I took pictures of me holding her hand — I had remembered DuJuan doing that with his father right before he transitioned, and I wanted that. I wanted a record of that last touch.

When Uncle Teddy and Auntie Nette arrived, we gave Uncle Teddy time alone with her first. Then we moved chairs into the room — enough for everyone. I was sitting on DuJuan's lap. And we just surrounded her. We started going down memory lane. We were laughing.

And then I noticed she wasn't breathing anymore.

We waited a few minutes. We called Nurse Kim.

At 12:54 a.m. on Monday, May 20, 2024, my mother took her last breath. She was surrounded by her people. She was pronounced at 1:37 a.m.

She died exactly the way she had always said she needed to. In her home. Surrounded by love. On her own terms.

She was, right up to the end, stubborn and unconventional.

The Chest That Wouldn't Open

Grief has a reputation for living in the eyes. In the tears. In the empty chair. In the reaching for the phone to call someone who is no longer there to answer.

What nobody told me is that grief also lives in the chest.

In the months after she passed, I was ambushed by it in ordinary moments — a holiday tradition, a piece of news I wanted to share, Elise telling me she'd gotten the internship she'd worked so hard for, and my first instinct being to reach for my phone and dial my mother, and then: the wall. That specific, wordless, physical wall.

The feeling was not sadness exactly. It was more like being punched — right in the sternum, right in the heart area — and finding that the air wouldn't come back.

With my mother's history of heart disease and my own struggles with hypertension, I couldn't afford to be careless. I began a carousel of medical appointments, trying to find a physical cause for the crushing sensation. My doctor on August 12. A stress test on August 27. A cardiologist on October 9. I sat in those cold exam rooms, thousands of dollars in medical bills accumulating, waiting for a diagnosis that would explain why my chest felt like it was being squeezed in a vise.

Every test came back the same: a clean bill of health. My physical heart was fine.

The pain remained.

In November, I wrote in my journal that the loss felt like my heart being slowly detached and *severed from my body with rusty children's scissors.*

I know that sounds graphic. I left it in because it was honest. That is what it felt like. Not a clean break. Not a surgical remove. The particular jagged awfulness of something being taken by the wrong tool.

The chest pain was love — forty-six years of it, condensed into a weight my sternum had to learn to carry. It was the cost of having loved someone that completely.

I would pay it again.

Clinging to 2024

On New Year's Eve, I sat down to write and said this to her:

> *A year ago today, I had no idea that you wouldn't be on this side of heaven. I didn't know that the last of everything we shared would be the last one we shared. I feel like clinging to 2024 simply because that was the last time you would be alive to share life with me. It's a completely selfish thought because I know that 2024 wasn't exactly kind to you. I just don't want to lose you. I don't want to leave you.*

I include that because it names a particular texture of grief that does not get talked about enough: the grief of crossing a threshold. Of entering a year, a month, a birthday, a holiday season that your person will never inhabit. Every *first* without them is its own loss layered on top of the original loss.

On January 1, 2025, I wrote in my journal: *"I feel like I've lost my sparkle. My light has been dimmed."*

I am not that woman anymore — or rather, I am not *only* that woman anymore. But I want to honor that she was real. She was me, five months out from the greatest loss of my life, sitting at the start of a new year she did not want, telling the truth about the darkness. That is how you begin finding your way back to the light.

Still Together, Just a Little Different

A scene from Moana arrived with unexpected weight. Gramma Tala's parting words to Moana rearranged something in me:

> *"Still together. Just a little different."*

I had to stop myself from weeping at a children's movie.

That phrase hit me like a revelation. It allowed me to shift my view from a place of *loss* to a place of *transition*. My relationship with my mother had not ended. The physical form of it had simply changed. She had moved to a different room in the house of my life, but the walls of that house still hold us both. We are still a team. She is still the Primary Architect, and I am still the builder.

The phrase "move on" has never felt like the right language for what grief asks of you. Moving on sounds like setting something aside and carrying on without it—and I am not setting my mother's memory aside. I am not setting the grief aside, or the lessons, or the years of preparation that looked like ordinary life. I am taking all of it with me. What I am doing—what this book is about—is moving forward. There is a difference. Moving forward signifies you are advancing and you are carrying what matters with you.

I still talk to her. I don't hear her voice in the answer the way I used to — that specific voice, that particular laugh, the way she had of saying my name when she was about to say something worth writing down. But I find her in other places. In the sign on the refrigerator that reads, *In the end it is good; if it is not good, it is not the end.* In the tenacity I feel when I sit down to do the work she would have cheered for. In the nonprofit being built in her name, in every pocket of time God makes available.

She is still here. Just a little different.

The Oxygen Mask, Repossessed

You know the airline briefing. In the event of an emergency, secure your own mask before assisting others.

My mother had been my safety net for forty-six years. She was the person who would catch what I dropped — emotionally, spiritually, sometimes practically. As long as she was downstairs, there was always a hand I could reach for. When she left, I was forced to face an honest question about myself: *How well have I actually been caring for my own heart?*

The answer was: adequately. Not well. *Adequately.*

I had been managing. I had been strong. I had been the woman other people called when they needed a steady presence. The grief cracked that open. Suddenly the feelings I had been filing neatly away had nowhere to go. They were in my chest, literally. They were in my body. The woman who was always composed was on the floor behind her desk at work, weeping, because she had finally run out of room to hold everything in.

I had to forgive myself for that. For the years of mistaking bracing for strength. For the times I had been too composed to be honest and too capable for my own grief to get a proper hearing.

The oxygen mask is not one single act. It is a whole practice — of becoming a woman who takes her own life seriously enough to steward all of it. The body. The grief. The rest. The calling. The relationships. The truth of how you actually are versus the version of yourself you've been presenting to the room.

For me, that practice looked like going back to therapy in earnest. It looked like taking a hike on Mother's Day 2025 and I am not a hiker — dragging my whole family along, because my spirit said I needed it and I finally knew enough to oblige. It looked like sitting down to write this book, which is to say: telling the truth on the page instead of filing it away.

My mother earned a beautiful death because people who loved her had the capacity to show up. I intend to be that kind of person — for Elise and Madelyn, for the people Cynthy's Kids will serve, and for the woman I am still becoming.

She left me her greatest lesson in her dying: *you cannot give from an empty place*. Fill yourself. Then give.

The key is to just keep breathing.

Day by day. Hour by hour. Or, minute by minute, if you need to.

But just keep breathing.

Who are you when no one's safety net is beneath you? Not who you present yourself to be — who you actually are, in the quiet, when the composure runs out and the real grief surfaces?

Grief does not stay in the mind. Where in your body does yours live? Your chest? Your shoulders? The catch in your throat in unexpected moments?

Have you given yourself permission to feel it fully — not to resolve it, not to manage it — just to let it be exactly as large as it is?

And where is she now — the person you've lost, or the version of yourself that left with them? Where do you still find them, even in the smallest places?

Write it down. You may find that what you are carrying is more than one loss. And you may find that what you call an ending is something else altogether — a different room in the same house. Still together. Just a little different.

____

____

____

____

CHAPTER FIVE

THE SACRED INDWELLING

*On the awakening that grief
makes possible — and the God
who was never absent.*

*"I AM is one of God's names. Whatever follows I AM
is a message to the Universe."*

— Cynthia Elaine Davenport, I AM Statements Are Packed with Power

I have found that you can survive something and still not feel strong.

After my mother died, people kept calling me strong. *"You're so strong." "I don't know how you're doing this." "You're handling this so well."* I would nod and thank them, but privately, I felt confused. I didn't feel strong; I felt tired. I felt suspended. I felt like I was moving because stopping would cause everything around me to collapse.

What they were calling strength felt more like momentum. I wasn't rising above anything; I was simply managing what was right in front of me. *Strong* implies certainty, grounded-ness, and an internal solidity I did not recognize in myself. I wasn't standing tall. I was functioning. And while functioning can look heroic from the outside, on the inside, it felt mechanical.

The Rearranging of the Soul

Grief rearranges the furniture of your soul—yes. But it also rearranges your sense of self.

After the gifted dinners stopped coming and the calls thinned out—after the paperwork was finished and the house returned to something resembling normal—I found myself facing a quieter, more structural question:

> *Who am I without her here guiding me, encouraging me? Who is this woman, and what is she capable of on her own?*

For years, my identity had been layered but stable: Wife. Mother. Daughter. Professional. Organizer. Planner. Executor. The roles remained, but something underneath them had shifted. The woman who had always called her mother for reassurance could no longer do that. The daughter who had been reflected back to herself through her mother's confidence no longer had that mirror.

She was my safety net—the one who held up a mirror to my strength when I couldn't see it myself, just as I had stood as her advocate through many seasons of her health journey. I have said it before and I will say it again because no single saying of it is enough: she was my shelter, my safe place, my sounding board, my home base, my salve for my soul. That daily connection was so deeply etched into my very essence that when it was severed, my body had no map for the sudden, heavy stillness.

Without that mirror, something subtle and significant happened: I had to see myself—not through her affirmation, not through anyone else's description of me, and not through the word *strong*. I had to see myself through my own recognition.

That was new territory.

The Woman Split in Two

What made it harder was this: I felt like I was being cut in two.

On one side was the woman my mother had raised me to be— faithful, grounded, capable, steady. On the other was the woman being overwhelmed by grief—disoriented, hollowed out, and moving through her days like she was wading through water. I had a hard time reconciling those two women. The one who was raised to keep going, and the one who had no idea how.

January 1, 2025 arrived and I wrote three sentences in my journal: *I felt like I had lost something essential—my light, my spark, the version of myself I recognized. I had never dreaded a new year before. But that one felt like a threshold I didn't want to cross—because crossing it meant leaving 2024 behind, and 2024 was the last year she was alive.*

I remember reading her refrigerator sign. *"In the end, it is good; if it is not good, it is not the end."* She wasn't there to say it to me anymore, but the refrigerator still was. And every single day, I read it. Cynthia Davenport was still speaking—she had just changed the medium.

The sacred indwelling is the chapter where those two women begin to reconcile — grief still present, something new growing alongside it.

The Fog Lifting

By December 2025, something had begun to shift. One afternoon I stopped and wrote down what was happening: Spirit has been unveiling things to me about myself — like a layer of thick fog being lifted by the breath of God, slowly, layer by layer, breath by breath.

Things I had never paused to examine — assumptions I'd been carrying, postures I'd maintained — were becoming visible. I wasn't always sure I liked what I saw. But at least I was seeing. And alongside the fog came something else.

In November 2025, I wrote this:

> *Every inhale is courage and resolve. Every exhale is fear and doubt leaving. I feel myself getting stronger.*

The Woman in the Mirror

There is a particular kind of quiet that follows crisis. The quiet of after. After the paperwork, the casseroles, the condolences. After the administrative competence that everyone around you praises as strength has finally done its job.

It was in that quiet that I began noticing her. Not my mother. *Me.*

One morning, weeks after everything had settled into its new routine, I stood in my bathroom longer than usual. I wasn't adjusting my hair or multitasking. I was just looking. The woman in the mirror looked like me. Her energy told a different story — restless, uncontained, unfulfilled.

For years, my identity had felt structured and secure. I was the planner, the executor, the one who handled things. Competence had become my currency, and it had served me well. But there was no steady voice on the other end of the phone to calibrate my thinking anymore, no one to confirm my instincts or say, *"Yes, that makes sense. You can do this."* Without that mirror, I finally had to see myself.

People still described me as grounded, strong, and stable. But internally, I was auditing.

> *What is my next step? What am I postponing? Where had I confused busyness with purpose—or humility with smallness?*

The Compression of Potential

The mirror does not lie when you stand still long enough.

What I saw was compression — years of it: the ambitious part, the visionary part, the part that wanted to build something structural rather than simply maintain what already existed.

I had convinced myself that contentment meant containment. That gratitude meant staying within familiar limits. That humility required shrinking.

There is a difference between collapsing and bracing. Bracing looks responsible. It looks steady. It looks like maturity. Often, it is simply fear disguised as discipline.

As I stared at my reflection, I recognized it. The set of my shoulders. The careful management of my own edges. I saw Little Liz in there—the four-year-old who had learned to stand still and stay quiet in a courthouse because the world felt too loud and too big to navigate. For her, bracing was survival. It was the only tool she had, and it held.

But the woman in the mirror was no longer that four-year-old.

The Locs

At some point, the interior shift demands an exterior one.

I had been growing my locs since I was pregnant with Elise — sixteen years of growth, sixteen years of identity. They were part of me that belonged to a particular season of my life. And sometime in November 2025, I found myself writing this:

> *I really feel like NOW is the time. I feel like even if I decide to regrow them later, they need to be regrown with new energy. These locs are old now. It's time for a change.*

I held that feeling for a few days. Then I wrote something sharper:

> *That's the reason for me wanting to cut my locs. I have to bury the old me that had a mom that I could depend on for any and everything. I have to grow past her and into a new woman. I now have to be the person that I needed from her, for my own children.*

There it was. Not a beauty decision. A burial. And a birth.

When my therapist found out I had already cut my hair—not that I was *considering* it, but that it was *done*—her eyes went wide. I showed her the picture of the bag of hair and she extracted a promise from me: no more changes. Not for a year.

I understood her concern. Grief counselors know that the body moves faster than the psyche can track. But I also understood something she couldn't see from her screen: my spirit had already decided. The locs weren't cut impulsively. They were released intentionally. The body was simply agreeing with what the soul already knew.

That is what transformation looks like from the inside. It was a quiet, irreversible act. The old season is over. I am not going back.

The Forgiveness I Owed Myself

The little girl in the courthouse had no other tools. Neither did the young woman she became — navigating grief and pressure and a life that kept requiring more. You cannot fault a person for using the only thing available to them.

But there comes a season when the bracing itself becomes the barrier. When what once held you together begins to hold you back. And in that season, you have a choice: you can keep defending the posture you've always known, or you can have the courage to release it.

I had to forgive myself for the years I spent small.

I had to acknowledge that I had been operating at a fraction of my actual capacity out of a fear. The woman in the mirror deserved to be released from the verdict she had been living under since a courthouse in 1982.

So, I released her.

It was a decision — the kind that happens alone in a bathroom before the world gets loud.

The Call I Had Been Sending to Voicemail

Something was waking up, quietly and persistently.

I had felt it before—in small stirrings, in restless seasons I had quickly filled with busyness. But the quiet after grief left me nowhere to hide. Watching my mother navigate her final years had removed my illusion of endless delay. And I knew: I could not keep postponing my own assignment.

God had been preparing me for something I kept refusing to see. I was paying attention — I was always paying attention. Agreeing with what He had been building just felt presumptuous. Too large. Like the kind of thing you say and then have to prove.

So I kept sending the call to voicemail.

There came a day when I finally sat with the question I had been avoiding: *What if everything I've been through was preparation?* The Boys and Girls Club. The twenty years of spreadsheets and attendance logs and systems built for other people. The administrative muscle I had developed without knowing why. The relationships formed in the steady rhythm of shared daily work.

What if God had been writing a résumé for me that I didn't know I had?

I couldn't answer that without sitting in it. Because agreeing with it would require something from me. It would require me to stop pretending I was only what I had always been. It would require me to start operating as the woman I was becoming.

That is personal responsibility of a different order. The kind that owns gifts as readily as it owns mistakes. The kind that looks at what God has been quietly building and says: I am not allowed to waste this.

The Sacred Indwelling

She got there first.

My mother had already written this theology before I knew I was living it. In an essay she never published, she wrote:

> *"I AM is one of God's names. Whatever follows I AM is a message to the Universe. Spirit accepts the statement as truth and proceeds to fulfill the statement."*

She wrote that. Cynthia Elaine Davenport wrote that. And somewhere, twenty-some years later, her daughter sat in the quiet of her own rearranged life and recorded these words into her phone:

> *I am in God. And God is in me. There is no separation. There is no distance. There is no space between us.*

Neither of us copied the other. We simply arrived at the same truth by the same road of a life that had demanded something real to hold on to.

This is what the sacred indwelling *actually* is. It is the living, cellular knowledge that you are not separated from God by your grief, your mistakes, your delayed obedience, or your years of smallness. He was in all of it.

This understanding that — I reside in Him, and He resides in me — stopped being a theological position and became the water I was living in. He had been here the whole time.

And then there was this: God had spent years making sure I knew that I could trust Him. Through every stepping stone, every divine appointment, every season that looked like nothing and turned out to be everything—He was building a track record. And I read it. I believed it. My faith in Him was not the thing I was struggling with.

What I was struggling with was trusting *myself*. The skills He placed in me. The instincts He had refined over twenty years of quiet labor. The woman He had been forming in the hidden seasons. I had faith in God, but I had been withholding it from her.

And I had to ask myself the honest question: if I truly believe that I reside in Him and He resides in me—if I truly believe that I am an extension of Him—then what does it say about my faith when I refuse to trust what He built?

I could not have it both ways. I could not claim the indwelling and treat everything He placed inside me as suspect. To doubt the gifts was to doubt the Giver. To shrink from the calling was to tell Him, quietly and consistently, that I did not actually believe He knew what He was doing when He made me.

That realization landed with the full weight of something I could not unfeel or unknow.

Trusting myself was not arrogance. It was not self-sufficiency. It was the final, necessary act of faith—the one that said: *I believe You. I believe what You put in me. I believe that when You said 'I reside in you,' You meant it. And I am going to live like it is true.*

Reporting for Duty

There is one more thing I want to say about the sacred indwelling. It is not passive.

It does not whisper, *sit still and wait for more confirmation.* It does not permit endless delay dressed up as humility. My mother wrote: *"I see myself as the unlimited, compassionate, loving, bold, creative, intelligent person God created me to become."* She wrote that while managing lupus, while living on disability, while doing the daily work of an ordinary Tuesday. She didn't wait to feel ready. She declared it—and then she moved.

The sacred indwelling is an invitation to do the same. To stand up in whatever room you're in—small frame or large, uncertain or confident, grieving or healed—and know that you are worthy of the space you occupy. You don't ask permission. You don't apologize for taking up room. You hold your head high and your back straight and you walk forward.

I was done bracing.

It was time to build.

Has there been a moment—a haircut, a decision, a quiet act of release—when your body agreed with something your spirit had already decided? What did that act say about who you were becoming?

And this: where are you still withholding trust from yourself? Not from God—you trust Him. But from what He built inside you? If you are truly an extension of Him, what would it look like to extend that same faith inward?

What calling have you been sending to voicemail? Not when you feel ready—but now, from exactly where you are?

PART III

THE STEWARDSHIP OF THE HIDDEN SEASON

> *"Preparation does not produce obedience automatically. I still had to agree."*

THE HIDDEN SEASON

On the preparation that looks like waiting — and the roots that were growing the whole time.

> *"Before a blade of grass breaks through the ground, the roots have to be nurtured, fed and watered."*
>
> — Cynthia Elaine Davenport, Spring Reflections

The question arrived quietly, the way the most disorienting questions always do.

It was February 13th. Nothing about the calendar marked it as significant. But I woke up afraid.

The vision for Cynthy's Kids had come quickly and persistently — weeks, not years — and it would not let me go. The bylaws were drafted. The paperwork was moving. And all of it — every bold, necessary, terrifying step — was pressing against a question I had been circling without the courage to ask it directly:

Who do you think you are?

The whispered kind. The kind that doesn't empower — it paralyzes. It lands right behind the sternum and settles there like a stone, dressed up just enough to sound like wisdom.

I sat with it. I let it name itself.

And then — God answered.

The Highlight Reel

What came next took my breath. God gave me a record — my own, twenty years deep. He set it before me and said: Read it. Read it the way truth deserves to be read — slowly, and without flinching. Because you have forgotten. And forgetting what I have built in you is not humility — it is waste. He let that land.

Then He began to play it back, one faithful season after another, each one finding its place in a story I hadn't known I was living. God's voice was clear:

> *"Girl, stop it. I've been preparing you for this for twenty years.*
> *You had been in your Master's degree program when you were in*
> *your early 20s. You put together a whole teen pregnancy prevention*
> *program in a high school on the rough side of town. You did that!*
> *You were in the newspaper to talk about what your program was*
> *about. You won a whole award for best practicum of the year in the*

> *Children, Youth, and Families sector! You've already done it, so you*
> *can do this again! I've been preparing you all this time; you just didn't*
> *know it. You thought that you were aimlessly wandering around*
> *going from spot to spot."*

That is what doubt does not survive: evidence. I watched the ordinary seasons of my professional life line up in a row and reveal themselves as something I had never once called them: preparation.

Not just "things I did". Evidence of what I could do.

I Thought I Was Just Doing Stuff

This is the part that still humbles me when I sit with it.

I spent twenty years in hidden-season labor. The May Department Stores, working in the COBRA department — learning customer service, how to manage offices, how to talk to human beings under pressure. The front desk at Acupuncture St. Louis and Wellness Center — learning how systems help run offices, how to hold a space with calm and competence. City Garden Montessori School, where I learned to put together programs and organize events and use spreadsheets as tools rather than tasks. The Fifth Grade Center, where God gave me room to breathe. And in that breathing space, consistency became character — ordinary days quietly shaping someone who could handle the extraordinary.

I thought I was just paying bills. I thought I was just being a responsible adult, filling roles, maintaining systems, keeping things running for other people. I did not understand — I could not have understood, from inside those seasons — that every single one of them was a classroom.

What the highlight reel showed me was confirmed by something I wrote to myself in September 2025, almost by accident:

> *"I noticed that when I started this journey, I didn't start from zero."*

That sentence stopped me cold when I read it back. I didn't start from zero. I never had. Twenty years of faithfully executed work had already been deposited into an account I didn't even know existed. When God called me to build Cynthy's Kids, He wasn't handing me a blank page. He was handing me a finished draft.

The Art of the Pivot

There is another kind of hidden-season labor that doesn't show up on a résumé. It happens in the side-hustle experiments, the creative detours, the seasons you file under "miscellaneous" because you can't yet see how they connect.

I made a note to myself in March 2025 that I called "The Art of the Pivot." It was a short entry — just a line, really — but it named something I had never allowed myself to acknowledge:

> *"Appreciate lessons learned from where you've been. Who knows what's still yet to come! Embrace it all!"*

What looks like an erratic career path from the outside reveals itself, from the inside, as a very consistent curriculum. Every pivot was practice. Every side hustle was a classroom that charged no tuition. Quixtar taught me something about entrepreneurship and independent operation. Photography trained my eye for seeing what others miss. Destination STL taught me logistics and client-facing service. Amazon Flex taught me self-management and real-time problem solving.

None of these felt like preparation. Each one felt like a detour, a side road, a thing I was doing while I waited for my real assignment to arrive. But the real assignment — building a nonprofit from scratch, with systems and vision and structure — quietly needed every single one of them.

The pivot is not the distraction from the breadcrumb trail. The pivot is the breadcrumb trail.

The Résumé God Was Writing

Specificity is what heals the doubt. Vague encouragement fades; evidence endures.

Here is what God had built in me across those twenty years:

> *A Master's degree from Washington University School of Social Work. A teen pregnancy prevention program, built from scratch, recognized publicly. A practicum award — best in the Children, Youth, and Families sector. Admissions Handbooks and Standard Operating Procedures created in buildings that had little structure before I walked in. Schoolwide events organized and sustained, year*

> *after year. Systems that outlasted my presence in the buildings that held them. The May Department Stores, Acupuncture St. Louis, City Garden, the Fifth Grade Center — each one a chapter in a curriculum I was writing without knowing it. Quixtar, Photography, Destination STL, Amazon Flex — each one a pivot that sharpened a skill I would need. Relationships built in the steady rhythm of daily work — friendships that became a fortress when the grief arrived.*

I had called these things ordinary for twenty years. I had held them lightly, as any humble person would. I had not understood that holding them lightly and dismissing them were two very different things, and that I had been doing the latter while believing I was doing the former.

Humility does not require you to pretend that God built nothing in you. In fact, refusing to acknowledge what God has built is not humility — it is ingratitude. It is looking at twenty years of faithful preparation and saying, "That doesn't count."

When the highlight reel played, I had to make a choice. I could keep dismissing the evidence in the name of modesty. Or I could do something harder: agree with it.

Agreement is different from arrogance. Arrogance says, *I built this.* Agreement says, *God built this in me, and I will not waste it.*

I agreed. Slowly. With a great deal of emotion I was not prepared for. But I agreed.

Hidden in Plain Sight

One of the most striking things God showed me during this season was that some of my deepest formation had happened through moments I didn't recognize as teaching at all.

There was a season when I was helping an older woman — her home, her business, the administrative layers of her daily life. And then one afternoon, mid-task, the Spirit said something I had to write down the moment it landed:

> *"Don't just do what she tells you to do. Pay attention to what she's doing. Get in the habit of doing these things so that you can do them for you and your family. She is teaching you how wealthy people handle their business. You better take notes and take advantage of this free training. In fact, she's paying you to learn it… literally."*

She was paying me to learn it. That reframe changed everything. What looked like service was actually enrollment. What looked like a side job was actually a master class. God had enrolled me in a curriculum and I had almost missed it because I was focused on the task instead of the lesson.

I have since learned to ask a different question in every ordinary moment: What is being deposited here that I haven't named yet? What is God teaching me in this room that I will need in the next one?

There was another entry I made around that same time — October 2025 — that I keep returning to: "Sometimes you have to slow down to speed up." I learned it during my Quixtar days, but most recently wrote about it in regards to a financial decision, a pivot in my strategy. But it named something true about the hidden season as a whole.

The years that looked like slowing down — the administrative work, the side hustles, the quiet seasons of simply showing up — were the conditions under which I was being accelerated toward what was next. You cannot rush the root system.

God's Delay Is Not His Denial

I wasted years not understanding this: God's delay is not His denial.

It is the law of the hidden season — the truth that makes the waiting bearable and the silence survivable. There were years when I felt like I was being left behind — years when the call felt real but the door wouldn't open, when the vision was forming but the provision wasn't there, when I couldn't see the next step and had no idea how any of it was going to unfold. In those years, I interpreted the delay as a verdict. I thought the delay meant no.

It didn't mean no. It meant not yet. And not yet meant the roots needed more time.

God designed the slow seasons. Every one of them. The breathing space at FGC was construction — He knew what was coming, and He was building what I would need to carry it. He was making me ready before I knew there was anything to be ready for. The flower does not grow faster by straining. It grows on schedule, in the conditions God prepared long before the bloom.

You do not need to know the how. That was the other thing the hidden season taught me, and it is the harder lesson of the two. I am a planner by nature. I need to see the map before I take the step. But

God does not owe me the map. What He offers instead is something better: His presence in the dark while the roots develop underground.

The flower does not ask how it will bloom. It does not negotiate with the soil or demand a timeline from the sun. It does not question whether it is growing correctly or whether it is growing fast enough. It simply does the only thing it was made to do — it grows, in the dark, before anyone can see it, trusting that the season for breaking through will come.

That is what I was doing in all those ordinary Tuesdays, in every spreadsheet, in every system I built without a nameplate, in every pivot that looked like detour. I was growing. I just couldn't see it yet.

Cynthia Planted This Metaphor Before I Grew It

She wrote about the flower first.

In an undated entry in her Spring Reflections — a personal spiritual journal she kept years before her passing — my mother wrote the words I quoted at the top of this chapter. "Before a blade of grass breaks through the ground, the roots have to be nurtured, fed and watered. The time it takes to develop the root system is time well spent, because those roots are the foundation for all future growth."

She was writing about spring. About rebirth. About the theology of second chances. But she was also, without knowing it, writing the exact truth that her daughter would need to receive decades later, when the hidden season felt too long and the doubt too loud.

She also wrote: "Every day can be spring."

Not every day feels like spring. She knew that. She had lived with lupus for thirty years by the time she wrote those words. She understood better than most what it meant to be in a season that didn't look like growth. But she also understood — in her body, in her faith, in the way she kept showing up every day — that the roots were doing their work even when she couldn't see it. The blade of grass would break through. It always had. It always would.

She planted the metaphor. I grew it. That is the breadcrumb trail across generations.

And in the spring of 2026, her daughter finally understood what she had always known: the delay was never denial. The quiet was never absence. The roots were doing their work, all along.

What the Doubt Was Actually Saying

Doubt rarely announces itself as doubt. It arrives as reasonable caution, as wisdom, as the voice of a person who is just trying to be responsible.

When the doubt said, "You don't have what it takes", what it actually meant was: "You have not yet taken full inventory of what you have."

When it said, "What if this doesn't work?", what it actually meant was: "What if you finally stop hiding and then people can see that you weren't hiding because you were modest — you were hiding because you were afraid?"

Fear of visibility is its own kind of ice block. I had spent so many years being excellent in the back rooms — building systems in spaces where the credit was collective, or where no one was watching particularly closely. I knew how to be quietly excellent. I was very good at it. And I had told myself for long enough that this was faithfulness, that I had begun to mistake the hiding for the virtue.

But God was not asking me to keep being excellent in the back rooms. He was asking me to bring the back-room excellence to a front-facing assignment. The work itself didn't frighten me. Two decades had made sure of that.

What frightened me was the standing. The being seen. The "having-my-name-on-it."

You have already done this. I showed you that you could. Now stop pretending you don't know how.

Doubt recalibrates when it meets evidence. It doesn't disappear. It just loses its authority.

What You Do With the Evidence

The highlight reel ended. The February 13th morning went on to become an afternoon, and then an evening, and then a night of paperwork and phone calls and the ordinary work of the life I am building. The fear did not disappear. The doubt has not permanently relocated.

I am still, some mornings, the woman who sits with the question: Who do you think you are?

But I am no longer the woman who has no answer for it.

The answer is the evidence. The systems still running. The programs still serving. The twenty years of faithful, quiet, unglamorous, extraordinary labor that God catalogued even when I didn't. The Art of the Pivot. The roots that were growing underground for decades before the blade of grass broke through.

When you review what God has built in you, doubt finds its proper place — shrinking from a verdict into a question you already have the evidence to answer.

You never started from zero. Neither did I.

The hidden season was preparation. The preparation was real. The delay was not denial. And the calling that awaits on the other side of it is not too large for what God has built in you.

The flower doesn't ask. It just grows.

And when the season shifts, it breaks through.

Looking back over your life — not just the highlights, but the ordinary seasons, the years that felt like nothing more than showing up — what has God been building in you that you have been calling "just work"?

Think about your own version of the Art of the Pivot: the side hustles, the experiments, the seasons you couldn't explain to anyone but you knew something was being formed. What did those seasons actually teach you? What skills, instincts, or character traits emerged from what looked like detour?

Write a list — not of your accomplishments, but of your capabilities. Not what you achieved, but what you became through the achieving. What do you know how to do because of the seasons you've walked through?

Now read it back.

That is the résumé God was writing while you thought you were just doing stuff. And the roots? They were growing the whole time. What becomes possible when you finally agree with the evidence?

____

____

____

____

CHAPTER SEVEN

THE STEWARDSHIP OF SILENCE

On releasing, receiving, and the grace it takes to do both

"Still together; just a little different."

— Gramma Tala, Moana — and then, somehow, also my mother

God Has Been Quietly Removing People

In January 2026, I sat with something that had been gathering weight for months. I wrote it plainly:

I feel like God has been slowly and quietly removing people from me.

I named them. One by one. Relationships that had grown quiet, grown distant, or grown cold without a clear explanation. Some I had known for years. Some felt mutual. Some simply stopped.

At first, it felt like isolation. Like something was wrong with me. Like the geography of my social world was shrinking, and I was somehow responsible for the disappearance.

But the longer I sat with it, the more I began to wonder if isolation was the wrong word entirely. Because there is another word. And that word is insulation.

> *Insulation preserves temperature. It protects what is forming. You do not incubate a vision in the open air — you shelter it.*

Isolation says: no one is here with you. Insulation says: this is a protected season, and access has been intentionally narrowed so that what is being built inside you is not disrupted before it is ready.

I was being prepared. And preparation is rarely comfortable — it often feels like loss before it reveals itself as provision.

The question I had to answer was not "What is wrong with me?" The question was: "Am I willing to trust that this narrowing is not punishment, but protection?"

Clutter is conversational, relational, emotional — not just physical. And God, who can see around every corner I cannot, sometimes removes it before we realize it was in the way.

Capacity and Compassion

There was a friendship — one I had valued — that had gone silent in a way I could not fully explain.

Some losses do not come with a funeral. No one brings food to your door. No one sends flowers or checks in a week later to see how you are holding up. The world does not pause for it, because the world does not always recognize it. But you feel it — in the body, in the pause before you realize the person you were about to call is no longer someone you call. A friendship that fades without explanation. A connection that simply goes cold. It does not announce itself as grief, and yet it sits in the same neighborhood. It has the same texture. The same ache. And I suspect I am not the only one who has felt almost embarrassed by how much it hurt — as if I did not have the right to call it grief over something that wasn't a death. But the hurt is real. The loss is real. And when you are already deep inside a season of undeniable, documented grief — the kind that does have a funeral, the kind that does bring people to your door — this quieter loss gets caught up in the current of it. Colored by it. Shaped by it. Made heavier than it might have been in any other season. What I was feeling toward this friend was happening inside the larger grief of losing my mother. It was not the same feeling. But it was in the same neighborhood. I did not have a name for it then. But I have one now.

What I felt toward this friend was tender. Grief-adjacent. Honest in a way that anger rarely is.

I understood, even as I sat with the sting, that grief changes us. I had watched it change me. There are things I said and did and did not do in the eighteen months after my mother died that I would handle differently now — not out of shame, but out of growth. Grief has a way of narrowing the aperture of what we can give and receive. It makes the world small, and sometimes it makes us small with it.

What I could not do was keep reaching toward someone who had stopped reaching back. She had her limitations in that season. I had mine.

I did not have the capacity, in that season, to carry my own grief and also carry the weight of someone else's grief with me. Love has limits, and honoring them is not a betrayal of it.

The oxygen mask is not a metaphor for selfishness. It is the architecture of sustainable care. You cannot breathe for someone else if you have stopped breathing yourself. I had been holding my breath in certain relationships for longer than I realized. And at some point, the body starts asking questions the mind has been refusing to answer

There is a particular kind of holding on that is easy to miss because it does not announce itself. It is quiet — the slow accumulation of what we have simply never set down. Nobody decides to hoard. We are simply not releasing. We hold onto the grief because at least it is familiar. We hold onto the connections because releasing them feels like another loss in a season already full of them. We hold onto their belongings — the sweater still folded, the handwriting on the notepad, the chair nobody sits in — because letting go of the objects feels like letting go of the person. And we are not ready for that. We may not be ready for a long time.

There is a difference, of course, between a memento and a museum. A memento is chosen — one thing kept because it holds something irreplaceable. A museum is everything, untouched, because the choosing felt too final. But eventually, even the objects ask to be released. And so, we carry all of it past its season, past its usefulness, past the point where it is serving us — because the alternative is an open hand, and an open hand feels terrifyingly close to empty.

But an open hand is not empty. It is available. And available is exactly what the next season requires.

What Little Liz Wanted to Do

People come into your life for a reason, a season, or a lifetime. Wisdom is knowing the difference — and having the courage to act accordingly, even when you wish the category were otherwise.

I will be honest about the part of me that did not want to let go.

Little Liz — the four-year-old who learned that her survival depended on not being left — had a very strong opinion about this situation. She wanted to run after the silence. To close the distance by any means necessary. To do whatever it took to ensure that the hand was still there, that she was not being abandoned again in the metaphorical mall.

She is very persuasive, Little Liz. She has decades of practice.

What I have learned, and am still learning, is that not every silence is abandonment. Some silences are choices. And when someone chooses distance — not because of crisis, or circumstances, but because they have decided the relationship no longer fits the life they are building — the most loving thing I can do is respect that decision.

Respecting it is not the same as agreeing with it. It is not the same as saying the hurt doesn't matter. It is not surrender. It is authority.

It is the adult woman saying to the four-year-old:

"I know this feels like the mall. I know your heart is doing that thing it does. But we are not going to chase this one. We are standing still. We are choosing purpose over pursuit. Because we know who we are."

Releasing with Love

My mother carried a saying attributed to Richard Bach that I have returned to more times than I can count:

"If you love someone, set them free. If they come back they're yours; if they don't, they never were."

I used to read that as a romantic sentiment. I understand now that it is a theology.

To release someone with love is not passive. It is one of the most active things I know how to do. It requires the deliberate decision that this person's journey is not mine to control, and that my peace is not hostage to their choices.

I wish her well. I mean that without decoration. The love I have for her is real, and real love does not require her presence to remain. I released the friendship, not the person. That distinction has mattered enormously to me as I've sat with it.

The thaw was already underway. This was part of it — releasing what no longer fit, making space in the hands for what was coming.

That clearing — that open space left by what I had finally set down — is where something else arrived.

It was June 15, 2025. My daughters were settled, the house was quiet, and we were watching Moana. When Gramma Tala reappears after her death — as a stingray, her spirit woven into the ocean she always loved — she finds Moana at her lowest. Lost. Unmoored. And she says:

> *"We are still together — just a little different."*

In the margin of my journal that same night, I wrote: Maybe this is how my perspective could change regarding my relationship to my deceased mother. We are still together, just a little different. I still talk to her. I just don't hear her voice in the answer. But perhaps it comes in other ways. Perhaps the strong breeze or the shining sun. Perhaps a gut feeling. Perhaps a whisper I can't trace to any earthly source. She is not gone. She is different. And the love between us did not end with her last breath; it simply changed its shape.

I tell you this here, in this particular order, because releasing what was leaving created the interior space to receive what that reframe offered. And that reframe — in turn — allowed me to finally see, with unclouded eyes, what had been standing right in front of me the whole time.

The Ones Who Were Already There

Here is what I did not fully appreciate until I stopped chasing what was leaving: I had already been held. For a very long time. By two women whose presence in my life is not accidental.

I have them categorized in my phone as my "A1s since Day 1". That label is earned. It is precise. Georgie and Tenay have been the backbone of my relational life for as long as I can remember. They both live in different states from me and different parts of the same state from each other. They cannot show up at my door with soup or sit beside me in a waiting room on a moment's notice. But distance has never once registered as absence with these two. Some friendships diminish with miles. These have only deepened.

Tenay and I met in the sixth grade. In seventh or eighth grade, there was a falling out — the kind that happens between young girls who haven't yet learned how to carry conflict with care. But even then, something in us knew better. Within a year or so, we found our way to forgiveness. No anger left, no animosity — just two teenagers who had done the quiet, unceremonious work of letting it go. The friendship didn't fully rebuild itself in that moment, and that's okay. We simply drifted, separately and without bitterness, into the rest of our adolescence.

What strikes me now is that we were already practicing what this chapter is about — releasing without resentment, wishing someone well and allowing the distance — long before I had the language for it. We forgave each other and God filed that away.

Our senior year, He brought it back around. As it turned out, we were both considering the same college. We both showed up — independently, without knowing the other would be there — for an overnight visit on the exact same weekend. I do not know what the statistical probability of that is. I know what I believe it was: a divine connection. God pressing two people back together who had been separated long enough.

We enrolled, got accepted, and became roommates our freshman year. And what had been an interrupted sixth-grade friendship became something rooted and lasting — sealed by a year of shared space, late nights, and the particular intimacy of two people figuring out who they are at the same time, in the same room. We have never lost connection again.

There is something irreplaceable about a friendship that was chosen twice — once before you knew what you were doing, and once when God made sure you found each other again. She has known every version of me, and she has never required me to perform any of them. When I became a mother, the question of who would be godmother to my daughters was not a complicated one. She was the right choice. A mama bear knows. And I knew.

Tenay is an accountant, which means she disappears into the holy intensity of tax season between January and April each year. And yet, in all the years I have known her, she has never been unreachable when it mattered. There is a difference between busy and unavailable, and she has always understood it.

This past March, she drove down to St. Louis alone, for no other reason than that it had been too long since we had been in the same room. She stayed less than twenty-four hours. She took me to my favorite restaurant, ordered my favorite dish, and quietly took care of the bill before I could say a word. It was a birthday dinner. It was also a friend showing up in the specific, unhurried, I-see-you way that some people are simply made for. We laughed and made fun of what growing older looks like in our lives, until our cheeks and stomachs hurt. I needed that more than I could have told her.

Georgie has been my ace since before I had the sense to know what an ace was. We met at Augustana College during the same trip that I reconnected with Tenay. She was already there when I arrived for that weekend visit, and what began as a college friendship deepened considerably when we became roommates for our junior and senior years. By the time we graduated, she was not just my best friend. She was family. She works now as an administrator in senior living, which means she has spent her career inside the tender, complicated geography of people's final seasons. When my mother's decline began, and I found myself navigating territory I did not have a map for, Georgie was the one I called.

She listened as I cried. She listened through the fear and the confusion and the specific grief that comes when you are watching someone you love begin to make their exit. She never rushed me, never minimized, never offered a solution when what I needed was an ear.

And then — gently, because that is how she does everything — she said something that rearranged me:

> *"Your mother is making decisions."*

She was not saying this to correct me or to close down the conversation. She was saying it to offer me something I desperately needed: a frame. My mother was not being taken. She was choosing. She was exercising the same agency she had exercised in every other chapter of her life — going back to school alone, leaving the job that no longer fit, building a relationship with her own father from scratch. The woman who had lived on her own terms was determining the terms of her departure. Georgie knew that. She had seen it before. And she wanted me to know it so I could stop fighting what was not mine to fight.

That one sentence did not take the grief away. Nothing does. But it changed the texture of it. It gave me somewhere to put my hands that was not resistance.

She spoke from experience — not just professional, but personal. She had lost her own father years before, and that loss had given her a tenderness and a precision when it came to this particular kind of pain. And she gave me everything she had from across a phone line, never once counting what it cost her to do so.

That March — when Tenay had driven down and Georgie and her husband came as well — the three of us were together for a stretch of hours that I will hold onto for a long time. It did something to my heart that I don't have a single word for. The best I can say is this: when the people who have known you the longest are in the same room, laughing and eating and simply being present, you remember who you are underneath everything that has happened to you. You remember the version of yourself that existed before the grief and the loss and the weight of the calling. And you understand, without anyone having to say it, that she is still in there. She always was.

And then there is the baby shower turnaround trip — Georgie, Tenay, and our dear friend Teressa making a same-day round trip, in and out, just to show up for that one afternoon. That is not a small thing. That is friendship in its most active form: present for the moments that matter, as much and as often as they possibly can be.

The stewardship of silence is not only about what you release. It is about what you tend. And I tend these friendships with everything I have — because they have tended me with everything they had, even in the seasons when I had nothing left to offer in return. Reciprocity is not a transaction. It is a commitment to keep showing up, in whatever form showing up requires — so that when someone else's season of empty hands arrives, you are already there.

Widen the Lens

There is a memory I keep returning to. There were good friends of me and DuJuan who live about forty-five minutes outside of the city — in the rural stretch of Missouri where there are no nearby buildings tall enough to drown out the sky.

I would go into their backyard at night and simply look up.

And the stars — the same stars I could barely see from our neighborhood — were spectacular out there. Bright and thick and so much more present than I had known they were. The sky was the same sky. The stars were the same stars. But the clutter had been removed, and suddenly I could see what had always been there.

That is what I am learning to do in this season: step back from the details I cannot control. Stop staring at the specific temperature and living conditions of each individual star. Trust that the stars are doing what stars are made to do — and focus on what I can actually see when I look up.

I only have control over me and my responses. Everything else — the choices others make, the silences they keep, the reasons they stay or go — that belongs to them and to God. My stewardship is not their behavior. My stewardship is mine.

The Road My Mother Built First

When I reached the edge of this work — when I finally started asking whether the distance between my father and me was something I was willing to keep carrying — I looked to my mother for a roadmap.

She had one.

Her own father had walked away when she was a baby. He returned when she was an adult, and what my mother chose to do with that still takes my breath away when I think about it. She did not pretend the abandonment hadn't happened. She did not perform forgiveness as a public gesture. She simply decided, from somewhere deep in the architecture of who she was, that the present relationship was worth more than the past resentment. She built something new with the man who had failed the child she had once been.

That was theology working in her own life. The same faith that refused to let illness become the headline. The same faith that left a stable job to go back to school alone. The same faith that sat on her refrigerator and said:

| *"In the end, it is good. If it is not good, it is not the end."*

She had applied it to her father. She was showing me, even from beyond her last breath, that I could apply it to mine.

I did not have to reinvent the wheel. I did not have to figure out from scratch what it looked like to hold the hurt of a father who had not been what you needed him to be, and still choose the relationship. She had walked that path already. She had left footprints. All I had to do was follow them.

The Father's Gems

My anger at my father had been circling me for a long time — the kind that lives in the body and flares at unexpected moments. The anger I had carried since the courthouse in 1982, when a four-year-old girl was asked to choose a parent.

That anger kept me from receiving things I actually needed.

He had introduced me to the concept of diversification before I'd ever heard the term. He taught me to "eat the meat and throw away the bones" — to absorb what gives you value and release what does not serve you and/or may cause you harm. He talked about not putting all your eggs in one basket.

I had been applying his wisdom for years. Watering seeds he had planted, without thinking about them being his. Because I was still holding the anger, I could never turn to him and say: I see you. I received what you planted. Thank you.

The anger was a block. And it was costing me something I did not yet fully know I wanted.

The Confession and the Truth

In September 2025, something happened that I had not planned and did not expect.

On that same call, I told my father that I appreciated him.

I told him I had been blinded by anger for a long time. I told him I was sorry I had not been able to see the things I was now seeing. I named the gems he had placed in me. I named the distance I had maintained and the false belief underneath it. I told him the relationship had always felt fragile to me, but that I loved him.

He received it in a way I had not anticipated. He was quiet for a moment. And then he said something that I have carried with me every day since:

> *"As parents, we do the best we can, in the season we're in, with the resources we have available."*

I held that sentence for a long time before I responded.

Because what he was offering me was not an excuse. He was not minimizing what I had experienced. He was offering me a framework — a way to hold his choices with grace rather than anger, even the ones I may never fully understand. That perspective belongs to me now — a woman who has herself been a parent, and knows what it is to do your best inside a particular season with whatever you have at hand.

He continued by saying that I might have less time in front of me than behind me — but that I have more life ahead of me than behind me. He said the memory is different from the mourning. I took that to mean that you cannot pick up the baton while you are still grieving. He closed with the words I had quietly made my own: 'The best is yet to come.'

I had heard that last phrase from the pulpit. As a salutation at the end of letters. A mantra that had quietly become part of my own interior landscape without my appreciating where it came from. He had been planting that seed in me for years. I had been watering it without acknowledging it was his.

Intention does not always override impact. A child who needed something and did not receive it in the way she needed it — that is real, and it does not require minimizing. But maturity allows us to hold both truths at the same time: the impact was real, and the intention was not cruelty. People do the best they can in the season they are in.

My mother had already proven that to me with her own father. Now I was living it with mine.

I am learning to see my father as he is — and the relationship between us as what it can be, rather than what it wasn't. That shift is a grace.

The reconciliation is ongoing — real, present-tense, and still unfolding. It is two people choosing the relationship that is over the relationship that wasn't. That, I have come to believe, is one of the bravest things a person can do.

Forgiveness as a Structural Decision

Sometimes, I think this gets lost when we talk about forgiveness in soft, spiritual terms:

Forgiveness is not a feeling. It is a decision. And it is one of the most structurally important decisions you will ever make.

I cannot build Cynthy's Kids while my hands are clenched around old hurt. I cannot lead a legacy with a heart that is still litigating the past. I cannot steward the relationships that are meant to last if I am spending my emotional capital trying to hold onto the ones that were never meant to be permanent.

Forgiveness is the act of freeing yourself — not absolution for anyone else.

When I released what was no longer growing, I was choosing peace over the right to be angry. I was choosing forward over frozen. And in that exchange, I cleared ground that I did not even know was occupied.

When I picked up the phone and told my father I appreciated him, I carried 1982 with me. The courthouse was still real. The four-year-old was still real. The wound that traveled with her all the way into adulthood was still real. And I chose, with all of that present, to see the man clearly — without the filter of the little girl's grief distorting the lens.

Both of those decisions cost me something. They required me to lay down the story I had been telling about my own pain. And they gave me back something larger: mobility. The ability to move without someone else's choices — or my own resentment of them — pulling at my heels.

I cannot build what I'm still bracing from. The thaw had to begin.

I did not have to wait for a sorry to start my yes. The yes was too important to hold hostage to the sorry.

Little Liz and the Unclenched Hand

Little Liz spent a long time with her fists clenched.

That was the only way she knew how to be safe. Hold tight. Hold on. Chase after the people who are walking away. Believe that if you lose them, you have lost something about yourself. Believe that silence means rejection, and that rejection means you were right to be afraid.

The adult woman I am becoming understands something that Little Liz could not: forgiveness is an act of authority. It is not surrender. It is not weakness. It is the moment I decide that my future is more valuable than my resentment, and that my peace is not for sale at any price — not even the price of being right.

The stingray moved through the water, and Gramma Tala said: We are still together, just a little different.

My mother is still with me. Different, yes. Changed in form, yes. But the love does not dissolve. The theology she planted does not disappear. The woman she raised is still standing, still learning, still becoming. And somewhere in that — in the summer stars over a rural Missouri backyard, in a September phone call where a father finally became visible, in a morning when I set down what I had been carrying too long — she is here.

The friendships that were supposed to last are lasting. The ones that were meant to be seasonal were seasonal. And the anger I carried toward my father since I was four years old — the anger that cost me decades of his wisdom — has been set down.

My hands are open now.

Take your time with these questions. They are meant to be held, not rushed.

1. *Is there a friendship or relationship in your life that has grown silent? How are you interpreting that silence — as rejection, as season, or as God's protection? What would it mean to see it differently?*

2. *Who in your life has been planting seeds you haven't yet thanked them for? What would it mean to tell them — while you still can?*

3. *Think of someone you are still carrying anger toward. What has that anger cost you — not in the abstract, but specifically? What could you receive if your hands were unclenched?*

4. *Georgie told Liz: "You're used to being there for others. Right now, I need everyone to be there for you." Who are your A1s? And are you letting them hold you?*

———————————————————————————

———————————————————————————

5. *Where in your own life have you confused isolation with insulation? What might be forming in you that needs protection, not exposure?*

———————————————————————————

———————————————————————————

∞ —— ∞

The next chapter turns inward — not toward what others have done, but toward the reckoning we owe ourselves. Because healing the relational is only part of the work. The other part is harder.

CHAPTER EIGHT

THE RECKONING

On owning what is yours — and setting down what was never yours to carry.

"Am I 'healing' or 'heeling' from my circumstance?"

— Elizabeth J. Harris, MSW, March 25, 2025

There is a particular kind of freedom that nobody warns you about.

The chapters before this one were the honest work of forgiveness and release. What comes next is something else — something that has your name on it in a different way.

I am talking about the other ledger — the one with your own name at the top. The one that asks, without cruelty and without mercy: What is yours to own?

This chapter is that reckoning.

The word deserves care before we go any further. A reckoning is the moment you open the books and look at what's actually there — without prostrating yourself on the floor, without rehearsing every mistake until you are sufficiently small. That is shame's work. And shame does not build anything. It seeks to destroy.

A reckoning is an accounting — an honest look at the numbers, all of them, including the ones you've been avoiding. You cannot build what you are called to build with a hand still pointing at someone else. And you cannot move forward freely while dragging the weight of things you have refused to name.

So, let's name them.

Two Kinds of Weight

In the courthouse in 1982, a four-year-old was handed a weight she was never supposed to carry.

She was told, in the language of institutional adults, that she had a choice to make. She carried that choice as if it had been a verdict. As if the divorce were something she had caused, or could have prevented, or was somehow responsible for not repairing. She carried it the way children carry the things adults drop — quietly, without complaint, because it seemed to be what the room required.

That weight was not hers. I have said it plainly in an earlier chapter, and I will say it here again because it bears repeating in this context: *she was not responsible for what broke. She was only responsible for surviving it.* And she did.

But here is what I have learned about false weight: carrying it for long enough trains the body to believe it belongs there. You stop noticing its presence because it has become part of your posture. You brace around it. You compensate for it. You organize your entire interior architecture to accommodate something that was never meant to be installed in the first place.

And then — when the hard, holy work of healing begins to strip away the things that were never yours — something unexpected happens. You feel lighter, yes. But you also feel, for perhaps the first time, the weight that actually *is* yours.

That is the reckoning.

It is real, it has your name on it, and it can actually be worked. In some ways, that makes it more manageable — because it requires you to be honest. It requires you to stop confusing the injury you survived with an excuse for the inaction you've chosen.

There is a difference between *because of what happened to me* and *despite what happened to me*. The first is a story I tell. The second is a life I build.

Patience With Her. Grace for Myself.

The moment I first understood the framework of this chapter, I was in the middle of one of the hardest nights of my life, in my mother's home, during the final days of her life.

My mother was agitated that evening. She said and did things that weren't her. And I lost my patience with a dying woman, and I felt the full weight of that the moment it happened.

DuJuan's words from that night had stayed with me: patience with her, grace for myself. I carried that framework into every season of accountability that followed, which required me to account for my own behavior without annihilating myself for it. Patience with the situation. Grace for the woman trying to navigate it.

That is not the same as excusing yourself. Grace is not a pass; it is a lifeline. It keeps you in the work instead of drowning in the self-condemnation that would pull you out of it. You cannot be accountable from a place of shame. Shame collapses you inward. Grace keeps you upright long enough to actually do the repair.

Patience and grace. I did not know it then, but that quiet instruction from my husband on one of the worst nights of my life was the accountability framework I would need for everything that came after.

The Ledger I Had to Open

I have already told you about the Boys and Girls Club. I did not dress it up when I told it in Chapter Three, and I will not dress it up here either.

I made a serious choice. It landed in legal territory. The consequence was community service, and I walked through the doors of that organization with my head down, carrying a shame I felt in my body.

But I want to tell you something I did not fully say there: the reckoning was not the court order. It was the moment I stopped pointing anywhere else and said, clearly and privately, to myself: I did that. That was mine. Fully. Permanently. Without the caveat of someone or something that made me or led me there. I was an adult. I made a choice. The consequence was fair. The grace that followed — the summer counselor role, the two years of formation, the young voice asking me if I still loved them — that grace was not earned by my regret. It was given despite my failure. But I had to actually own the failure before I could receive the grace.

You cannot receive what you have not made room for. And you cannot make room while your hands are still full of excuses.

The ledger had other entries, too.

For years, I knew God was calling me toward something more. I could feel the stirring. I just did not know its shape. I thought, for a long time, it might be a children's book — a series of life lessons, something that would outlast me in a small but good way. I had no idea I would be writing this. I had no idea about Cynthy's Kids. Even when the vision came, in January of 2026, it felt at first like a beautiful dream set somewhere off in the distance. It was not years of ignoring a clear assignment. The assignment became clear in weeks — and the speed of that clarity was exactly how I knew it was God-led and not self-generated.

But I can tell you honestly: there were seasons when I had the *stirring* and I sent it to voicemail anyway. Where I dressed avoidance as patience and called delay a season. I wrote it to myself once, plainly, in the quiet of my own journal: *In the deep recesses of my mind and heart, I don't really think I can do these things. So, I don't even try.*

Then I stopped. And I wrote what I thought of that admission:

> *That is tragic. And I am the only one who can fix it.*

That moment was a reckoning — raw and uncomfortable, but honest. And honest is what moves you forward. Honest is what breaks the resistance line.

Owning a specific mistake is one kind of reckoning. You can point to it. It has a date, a shape, a before and after. The harder kind is owning a pattern — the quiet, accumulated habit of naming everything else instead of naming the fear underneath. The timing. The season. The conditions. A thousand small decisions, each reasonable on its own, adding up to a direction you did not consciously choose.

But it is still yours. And until you own it, you will keep explaining it.

Healing or Heeling?

On March 25, 2025, a question came to me that I couldn't shake. It sat in my chest like a disturbance I hadn't asked for. I wrote it down:

> *Am I 'healing' or 'heeling' from my circumstance?*

They sound almost identical. They are not.

Healing is active. It moves through the pain toward something new. It requires you to look directly at the wound, name it, feel it, and then make the daily decision to tend to it rather than protect it. Healing is hard, it is not linear, and it does not arrive on a schedule. But it is always moving — always oriented toward the light, even when the steps are small.

Heeling is something else. Heeling is what a dog does when it has been trained to walk obediently just behind its owner — never ahead, never free, always in the shadow of something that came before. When I am heeling from my circumstance, I am following the injury. It is still setting the pace. I am still organized around it, still making decisions in reaction to it, still allowing it to determine how far I can go and how fast I am allowed to move.

Healing and heeling can look very similar from the outside. Both are quiet. Both are slow. But one is moving forward and one is being held in place by the leash of the past.

The reckoning asks you to be honest about which one you are actually doing.

Treat it as information. Because if you are heeling, the moment you name it is the moment the leash loosens. You cannot walk free of something you have not acknowledged is still attached.

I have done both. There were seasons when I thought I was healing and I was heeling. There were seasons when the grief, the anger, the old wound was still setting the terms of my life — still determining what I reached for and what I left on the table — and I was calling that faithfulness or patience or wisdom. Sometimes it was those things. And sometimes it was heeling dressed up in spiritual language.

The difference, I have found, is motion. Healing moves — even slowly, even painfully, even two steps forward and one step back. Heeling holds still and waits for the wound to give you permission.

I stopped waiting for permission.

Lessons Are Repeated Until Learned

My mother was one of the wisest women I have ever known. She could see around corners for other people with extraordinary clarity. She counseled friends with precision and love. She had the words for almost everything.

And then I read her journals.

I found, in her own handwriting, the evidence that the lessons she taught others were the lessons she was still learning herself. The wisdom she dispensed so freely in one direction was the wisdom she could not quite apply in another. I did not read those pages with judgment — I read them with recognition. Because I know what it is to see clearly in someone else's situation what you cannot yet see in your own.

She used to say, *"You teach people how to treat you."* She said it like a woman who had learned it the hard way and wanted to spare me the same tuition. Lessons are repeated until learned. You either graduate the lesson by owning it, or you re-enroll — same material, different teacher, and a tuition that only gets more expensive the longer you wait.

I received that lesson. And then I had to ask myself, with the same unflinching honesty my mother would have wanted for me: *In what areas of my own life have I been re-enrolling in the same lesson? Where have I been teaching people that certain things are acceptable, by accepting them? Where have I been waiting for someone else to change so I could begin?*

That is a question only you can answer for yourself. I will tell you what I found when I answered it for myself: the places where I felt most wronged were often the places where I had been most passive.

Where I had hoped rather than communicated. Where I had waited rather than moved. Where I had been very busy being a student of my injury and not quite busy enough being a student of my responsibility.

Owning that did not mean the injury wasn't real. It was real. Both things are true. The thing that happened was real. And my response to it — or my failure to respond — was also mine to own.

That is the full picture. Not comfortable. But full.

My mother also wrote something that I return to often from her own private essays, which I have begun reading now that she is gone. She wrote about the stewardship of the mind with a clarity that stopped me cold: *"When I stopped engaging in self-depreciating thoughts, my experiences changed. In a really good way!"* And separately: *"Take charge of your life! You have the power to make it whatever you want it to be."*

The woman who modeled faith for me before I had language for it wrote the stewardship of the mind chapter before I was old enough to understand what it meant. And now I am her daughter, living it out in real time — doing the thing she described, becoming the proof of what she planted. That is the difference between a lesson received and a lesson owned.

Little Liz in the Ledger

Little Liz learned two things in that courthouse that she was not supposed to learn.

The first is the one I have already named — that she was responsible for what broke. The verdict on that entry reads: *not guilty. Never was.*

The second lesson was quieter and more stubborn: Little Liz learned to brace.

In the courthouse, bracing was the right response. Stand still. Stay quiet. Survive the room. That four-year-old girl had no other tools, and the ones she made do with were exactly sufficient for getting her through. I will not fault her for that.

But bracing, when it becomes the default posture for everything that follows, looks like something it is not. It looks like patience. It looks like steadiness. It looks, from the outside, like a woman who has everything under control. What it actually is is a woman waiting for the room to become safe enough before she moves. Waiting for the conditions to settle. Waiting for the uncertainty to resolve. The brace that held Little Liz together in the courthouse quietly became the reason the adult woman moved slowly into rooms she was already built for.

Nobody was coming. The woman in the mirror had to . She had to step forward from behind the story of what happened to her and pick up the assignment that had been waiting.

This is not a criticism of Little Liz. She was surviving. She did exactly what she needed to do to get through.

But part of the reckoning — the full reckoning, the one that actually opens the door to the next season — is setting her down. Not abandoning her. Not forgetting her. Not closing the door on her. But finally, lovingly, clearly saying:

> *You carried what you could carry. You survived what you needed to survive. The courthouse is not home, and we are not going back. It is time for the adult woman to lead now. You are safe. You are loved. You are free. And you do not have to protect me anymore.*

That is what Little Liz needed to hear — and what finally allowed me to step fully into my own accountability without confusing it with punishment. I am not being held responsible for what happened to her. I am being freed to own what I am choosing from here.

Forgiveness Completes Here

In the earlier chapters of this book, forgiveness arrived in stages.

I forgave others — or I began the work of it. I named the relationships I was releasing. I named the father I was choosing to see new. I gave the pain back to the One who could actually do something with it. That is real, and it is necessary, and I do not minimize it.

But forgiveness has a second direction — and in this chapter, it stops being peripheral and becomes central.

I had to forgive myself.

Fully. The version where you look at the choices you are not proud of, the seasons of delay, the moments where you were small because it was safer than being seen, the patterns you inherited that you kept longer than you should have — and you say:

> *I forgive the woman who did not know better. I hold accountable the woman who does. And I refuse to let shame use the one to paralyze the other.*

Forgiveness without accountability is permission. Accountability without forgiveness is punishment. What God is asking for is both — the full release of the past and the full ownership of the present. The two together are not contradictory. They are the architecture of a free life.

Forgiveness completes here — in this room, where you look at your own ledger and say: I see it. I own it. I am not defined by it. And I am moving.

The Work, Daily

Owning your ledger is a daily practice. And a daily practice requires a daily environment.

I have a choice and I choose me. My sanity. My peace. I wrote that to myself in November of 2024, in the middle of grief and noise and a world that felt like it was spinning off its axis. I meant every word — and then I had to build a daily life around it.

This is what that started to look like in practice: I turned off the television. Five to six hours of news every evening had been filling the space where my own thoughts should have lived. I replaced it with audiobooks that built me up, with music chosen for what it moved toward, with podcasts that fed the direction I was trying to grow in.

I watched the words that left my mouth, because I had learned that what you speak has a way of becoming what you believe. I became a gatekeeper of what my eyes consumed.

It was quiet, consistent, and entirely within my control — which is exactly why it mattered. The reckoning had cleared the room. These habits were how I decided what to put in it.

I also went back to therapy — because construction requires someone who can read the blueprint with you and tell you honestly when something is not load-bearing. That is what therapy was. Evidence that I was taking the rebuild seriously.

What I came to understand is that the space in your mind is precious real estate. Whatever you allow to move in there — rent-free, uninvited, defaulting to whatever the loudest screen in the room is playing — shapes the internal loop of ideas and thoughts you will be living inside of all day. That loop is either fuel or drag. There is very little in between.

Personal responsibility does not end with the acknowledgment. It extends into every small daily decision about what you let in. What you watch. What you read. What you listen to on the drive to work, in the hour before bed, in the quiet moments when the noise of the day has finally settled. These are not peripheral choices. They are the practice of becoming the woman you just agreed to be.

I have also watched people around me confuse busyness with productivity — and the confusion is an easy one to make. Busyness feels like progress. It looks like effort. But a full calendar is not the same as a fruitful one. Productivity moves something forward. Busyness can simply be motion without direction — the appearance of work without the advancement of purpose. The reckoning eventually asks you to tell the difference.

Busyness is often the loudest tenant. You cannot do the interior work of the reckoning and then hand the keys of your mind back over to whatever is loudest. That is not stewardship. Stewardship of what you let in is part of the same assignment as owning what you let out. Both are yours. And both, done faithfully, will move you forward.

The Gateway

The other side of a reckoning is the freest you have ever been.

When you are carrying false weight, you expend energy managing the carrying. When you are carrying real weight that belongs to you but refusing to acknowledge it, you expend energy managing the avoidance. Both are exhausting. Both are invisible drains on the capacity you need for the life you are being called to build.

The reckoning clears the room.

The process is neither painless nor quick. But it is complete. When you have stood in that room and said — with the same honesty you extended to your own story of survival — this is mine, and this is not, and I am setting each one down in its proper place — you walk out with your hands free.

And you need your hands free. Because what God is asking you to build requires both of them.

You cannot serve your calling with your energy split between forward momentum and backward resentment.

You cannot be the woman you are becoming while you are still managing the woman you are hiding.

I know this because on February 27, 2025 — my 47th birthday, one week out of surgery, nine months after saying a final goodbye to my mother — I sat down to write in my journal and something had shifted. The hole was still there. She was still gone. But I wrote something that surprised me:

> *I feel like it just gets better from here. I feel like my why is being cemented firmly into my backbone. I feel like I get better and better as I get older.*

That is what begins to feel possible — the first glimpse of a woman whose hands are starting to open, whose backbone is starting to solidify. Something that feels, against all odds, on a birthday in February, like the beginning of joy.

The reckoning is where the prologue ends and the story begins. The story of what you chose to do with it.

I am doing this work. It does not happen once, in a single chapter, on a single morning. It begins with the willingness to open the ledger — to look at it honestly, to own what is there, and to name it.

And then — to close it. Completely, and with intention.

> *The courthouse is not home. It never was. This is the declaration of departure.*

The breadcrumbs continue. And from this chapter forward, the woman following them is walking with her hands open.

≈ —— ≈

Am I healing or heeling right now? What would it look like to choose healing — fully, today?

And then: *What have I been waiting for someone else to fix that is actually mine to own?*

It is counterproductive to do this in blame or shame. Just be honest in your assessment.

Take a moment. Write it down. Not the story of what happened — you have already told that story, and it deserves to be told. But the part of the story that belongs to you: the season of delay, the pattern you kept, the inaction you dressed up as patience, the excuse that became a way of life.

Write it. Name it. Own it. And then — this is the important part — write what becomes possible on the other side of owning it.

Because something does. Something always does.

The reckoning is not the end of the story. It is the first sentence of the next one.

____

____

____

CHAPTER NINE

THE LAW OF ALIGNMENT

Alignment is not a passive state. It is a synchronized movement — and the walking is yours.

"I co-create those dreams with God. It's a divine relationship — a sacred covenant."

— Cynthia Elaine Davenport, April 2017

There is a difference between being ready and being willing to move.

I had been ready for a long time. Ready in the way a runner is ready at the starting line — weight forward, breath controlled, body primed by years of training. The preparation was genuine. The hidden season had done its work. The highlight reel had been played back to me on a February morning until I had no honest argument left against it. Twenty years of what I had called *ordinary* had been revealed as extraordinary formation. I had no rebuttal.

What I had not yet done was answer the bell.

There is a version of faith that looks like faithfulness but is actually paralysis. It speaks the right language. It prays the right prayers. It even believes — genuinely, wholeheartedly — that the calling is real and the season is turning. And then it waits. It waits for the conditions to settle, the doubt to clear, the path to announce itself with enough certainty that stepping onto it feels safe.

Mature faith does not wait for safe. Mature faith moves.

The Bell

In my years working in school buildings, I came to understand the bell as an authority unto itself. It does not ask. It does not negotiate. It rings — and the room responds. You do not argue with the bell. You do not petition it for a few more minutes to finish what you were doing. The bell says the season has shifted, and the only question remaining is whether you are ready to acknowledge it.

By 2025, God's bell had been ringing for a while. I could hear it. I could feel it in the urgency that had begun settling into my spirit — the kind of urgency that is not anxiety but something more like a righteous impatience. The vision for Cynthy's Kids was no longer just a stirring. It was becoming a structure. The legal work was being drafted. The conversations were beginning. The walls were going up even as the doors were not yet open.

The bell was ringing. And I had to decide: report for duty — or keep sending the call to voicemail.

Mature Faith and Immature Faith

I want to give you a distinction that changed something in me when I finally saw it clearly, because I think it is one of the most important dividing lines in the spiritual life.

Immature faith says: *God will handle it.* It uses prayer as a substitute for participation. It sits at the gate, dressed in the language of trust, waiting for God to move when He has already positioned you to move with Him. It looks devout. But underneath, it is avoidance — waiting to be moved rather than choosing to move.

Mature faith operates by a different law. It says: *God will guide it; I will steward it.* It understands that He provides the breadcrumbs — and the walking is ours. He provides the direction; we provide the movement. He provides the capacity; we provide the discipline. He opens the door; we actually walk through it.

Alignment is not a passive state. It is a synchronized movement. You cannot synchronize with a direction you are not moving in.

My mother said it in her own language, in 2017, in a document she wrote for herself: "I co-create those dreams with God. It's a divine relationship — a sacred covenant." She was not waiting to be handed her destiny. She was co-creating it. She is the Primary Architect — not only of my faith, but of the theology I am now living out.

The Expiration of a Season

I have learned to read frustration differently than I once did.

There was a time when frustration meant something was wrong with me — that I was impatient, ungrateful, or failing to trust the process. I now believe almost the opposite. In the right context, frustration is not a character flaw. It is a signal. It is the body and the spirit together saying: *this season has reached its edge.*

At City Garden Montessori School, I had been formed in ways that were genuine and irreplaceable. I learned what it means to build from very little — to create programs and systems and a welcoming presence in a place that had little infrastructure before I arrived. I learned to be the face that families met first, the voice that said *you are in the right place*. All of that was real, and I carry it still. But there came a season when the frustration I was carrying could no longer be managed into quiet. It was no longer asking me to be patient. It was asking me to *move*.

In the past, Little Liz might have chased a resolution. She might have adjusted herself, explained herself, tried one more time to make the fit work in a room that had become too small for the woman she was becoming. But I had done the reckoning. Little Liz had been set down with love. And the woman who picked up the phone that evening was not bracing. She was clear.

I called my friend Darcell.

There are people in your life who are not cheerleaders — they are *seers*. Darcell is one of mine. She does not offer comfort as a default. She offers clarity. She knew my season before I had fully named it, and when I described where I was, she did not tell me to wait it out, pray it through, or give it more time. She cut straight through it:

> *"Get your laptop. We're about to find you a new job."*

No preamble. No hedge. Just direction. A friend with a laptop and the authority of someone who has been watching God prepare you and is simply done watching God's gifts being wasted.

The Two-Week Acceleration

What happened next is the evidence I return to when doubt starts building its case.

I applied for the Registrar position at the Ladue School District — a role I had not been strategically targeting, had not read the full description for, had not built a campaign around. What I had done was show up. I applied. I reported for duty.

Two weeks. From application to interviews to board approval to the moment I could officially announce I was the new Registrar for the Fifth Grade Center — two weeks.

That acceleration was not coincidence. It was confirmation. It was what the hidden season had been building toward and what the reckoning had cleared space for: evidence that when you stop sending the call to voicemail and step into alignment with God's timing, the breadcrumbs do not just continue. They become a paved highway.

I did not have to beg for that position. I did not have to manufacture the right conditions or force a door that was never mine to open. I had to be ready — which I was, because twenty years of formation had made me ready — and I had to move when the door opened. That was all.

But I want to name something plainly, because I think this is where so many of us stay stuck: readiness and willingness to move are not the same thing. I was ready for years before I was willing. The hidden season built the capability. The reckoning cleared the room. Alignment required me to actually walk through the door.

You can carry the résumé God has been writing for you and still call it *just a job*. The law of alignment is simple: you have to agree. Now.

When God Cancels the Appointment

I want to give you the other side of the two-week acceleration, because I think it is just as important and considerably more common.

Not every door swings wide on your timeline. Sometimes alignment looks like a cancelled appointment, a morning of phone calls, and the particular sting of having done everything right — and still watching the plan fall apart.

I had been intentional about everything. I gathered every document. I coordinated the co-signer's schedule. I spent time the night before choosing my outfit with purpose, because I understood that this meeting mattered — that the founding of Cynthy's Kids deserved to be met with that kind of seriousness. I submitted the paperwork as early as I could get it in. I had my questions ready. I had done the work.

And on the morning of the meeting, I learned the appointment had to be cancelled. The bank representative had left early the day before without retrieving the documentation I had submitted. Without back-office approval, there could be no meeting. The date I had been holding, coordinating around, building toward — was gone.

I was angry. I was frustrated. I was disappointed. The sanitized version of faith — where a woman of God receives disappointment with immediate, serene acceptance — is not the version that actually helps anyone. The real version is: I did everything I was supposed to do, and it still fell apart, and I had to sit with that.

This was supposed to be a significant day for Cynthy's Kids. And it was not. And I had to feel that before I could release it.

But after the anger had moved through me — after the frustration had been acknowledged rather than suppressed — I came to a truth I already knew intellectually and now had to choose: God's delay is not His denial. All things happen in His timing. His will is the only one worth following. And I had to become okay with things not happening in my timing.

I do not know why that day was not the day. Maybe there was something waiting to be corrected in the process first. Maybe there was a protection in the delay I will only understand later — or never. God sees around corners I cannot see. He knows the future of whatever is unfolding. And the thing I have had to practice accepting is this: I am not always entitled to the explanation. I am only entitled to the trust.

That day was not the day God wanted us to do it. And therefore, we didn't. And we have to be okay with that. That is not resignation or defeat. That is the most mature form of faith I know how to practice: releasing the grip on my timeline without releasing the commitment to the vision.

The two-week acceleration and the cancelled bank appointment: one showed me what alignment looks like when God swings the door open. The other showed me what it looks like when He holds it shut — and why both require the same response.

Trust the One who sees around the corner. Release the emotions — feel them fully, then release them. And keep moving. God's will be done.

City Garden Prepared My Face; the FGC Showed Me the Standard

I want to speak specifically about what those two roles gave me, because the sequence matters — and I would waste the lesson if I passed over it quickly.

City Garden prepared my face and put tools in my hands. It trained me to be present, organized, welcoming, and the one who makes the threshold feel like an invitation. It was also where I built without a blueprint: programs written where none had existed, handbooks developed, events organized in a building that was still finding its form. I learned what it means to start with very little and make something worthy.

The Fifth Grade Center showed me what excellence looks like when it is already fully built. The systems there were not improvised — they were the gold standard. My job was not to create; it was to *learn, maintain, and understand* that blueprint deeply enough to carry it forward. Every SOP I internalized, every infrastructure rhythm I kept running, every process I stewarded at that level of precision — God was showing me the standard I would one day be expected to replicate.

When the vision for Cynthy's Kids arrived, it did not arrive shapeless. It arrived with a skeleton, because I had spent years studying what a skeleton at its best is supposed to look like.

Had I stayed at City Garden in my frustration — had I managed myself smaller and refused the alarm my spirit was sounding — I would have missed the second formation entirely. I would have arrived at the calling without the blueprint.

The breadcrumbs knew exactly where they were going. They always do.

The Final 400 Meters

In high school, I ran cross country for a short time. I was not a distance runner by nature, but I learned something during that time that I have never forgotten: the last stretch changes everything.

When you have been running for miles — when your lungs have done the long, disciplined work of the middle distance — something shifts in the final 400 meters. Not in your body, exactly, but in your will. The finish line becomes visible, and something that had been moving through you at a steady, managed pace suddenly has permission to *surge.* You pick up the pace. You pump your arms. You control your breathing with a different kind of intention. You are not running the same race you were running a mile ago. You are finishing it.

By September of 2025, I could feel the final 400 meters approaching.

I wrote it plainly in my journal, because that is how it arrived: *There is no time for hesitation. The time for self-doubt, confusion, and distraction is OVER. The final 400 meters are in sight. It's time to sprint to the finish line. Kick up those knees, pump those arms, control your breathing, and FINISH STRONG. That's the only outcome there will be, because God is my strength.*

I knew I was working seven days a week. I knew I was not getting younger. I knew that the window of full capacity was limited. My mother used to say you can do anything for a short amount of time. I believed her. And I knew this was my short amount of time.

That kind of urgency is not fear. Fear makes you freeze. This urgency made me *move.*

Must-ness

Around the same time, two things arrived on the same August day, which I now understand as God doubling down on a message He had already spoken.

First, my husband's cousin preached a sermon in Oklahoma about what he called "must-ness" — the steadfastness of doing God's will.

Not the willingness to obey when conditions are favorable, but the burning, irreducible sense that you *must*. When you know that grace pulled you out and God's mercy carried you through, you don't have the luxury of delay. You move on the word of the One who sent you. *My life is not my own.*

That same day, I picked up a book that delivered the same message in an entirely different voice. My father used to say: *eat the meat, throw away the bones.* The meat of that book was this: you are not what you think. You are what you do. Make the choice that deploys the doing.

Two breadcrumbs on the same day, pointing in the same direction. That is not coincidence. That is God confirming what He has already said.

I expected must-ness to feel like pressure. It felt more like clarity — the specific stillness of a woman who has stopped arguing with what God has already told her.

Achievement vs. Fulfillment

In January 2026, I watched someone I love, respect, and admire make a decision that clarified something I had been turning over for months.

Dr. Wilson — a woman I have seen lead with integrity, warmth, and the kind of authority that comes from genuine care for people — made a choice many people around her did not understand. She decided to leave a thriving school where she had built something real to return to a much different environment with fewer resources. Compensation was not her focus. It was about mission. It was about following what she believed God's purpose for her life and career actually required.

Many people read that as a step backward. I read it as alignment.

The distinction between *achievement* and *fulfillment* matters more than I can fully explain in a single chapter. Achievement asks: *what have I built?* Fulfillment asks: *am I building what I was made to build?* You can have one without the other. A career can be successful by every external metric and still feel like something you are managing rather than something you are *living*.

Alignment is what closes the gap between those two things. It is when the work you are doing is the work your soul agreed to. It is when you stop achieving for achievement's sake and start building for *purpose's* sake.

I want that kind of clarity. Watching Dr. Wilson choose her calling over her comfort reminded me that it is not only possible — it is the only thing worth choosing. The final 400 meters are in sight. I am running toward fulfillment, not just achievement.

The Pain of Discipline and the Pain of Regret

My mother used to say something I heard as instruction and now understand as strategy.

> *"You either pay now or you pay later. But everyone pays."*

She was not just talking about money — though she was right about money too. She was talking about parenting. About consequences. About the choices you make when the cost is still small, versus the choices you make when the cost has compounded into something that cannot easily be undone.

I have known both kinds of pain. The pain of discipline is acute. It interrupts comfort. It demands structure when ease is available, consistency when postponement is technically possible. It hurts in the moment, and in the moment, the hurt feels unnecessary.

The pain of regret is quieter at first — barely detectable, easy to rationalize, patient. It does not announce itself as pain in the early stages. It simply accumulates. And then, somewhere in the life you built by always choosing the easier path, it surfaces — the full weight of the roads not taken, the assignments sent back to voicemail one too many times.

Regret compounds. And unlike discipline, it does not sharpen you. It erodes you.

In this season — Cynthy's Kids becoming real, systems being built, legal work filed, boards forming, this book being written in the margins of a life that is already full — I have chosen the discipline. I have worked multiple jobs while writing at night and building in the early morning hours. I am paying the tuition of now. I will not arrive ten years from now wondering what would have happened if I had committed fully. I have already spent years wondering. That account is closed.

The discomfort of discipline sharpens you. The discomfort of regret erodes you. My daughters are watching. I choose the pain that refines me.

Sovereignty and Stewardship

I used to believe that trusting God meant letting go — that surrender was the whole assignment. I have come to understand it as half.

God is sovereign over the impact. He is not waiting for my participation to move things into position. The February 13th highlight reel was not assembled by me. He had been cataloguing every faithful ordinary Tuesday for two decades without my awareness or help. His sovereignty is not in question.

But I am responsible for my response. I cannot pray away poor preparation. I cannot hope miscommunication resolves itself. I cannot wait for confidence to arrive before I act as if I have it. Cynthy's Kids did not materialize because I believed it into existence. It materialized because I *acted* on the belief — researched, drafted, structured, showed up, and kept going when the going was slower than the belief had promised.

My mother understood this. She wrote it years before I found my own language for it: "I co-create those dreams with God. It's a divine relationship — a sacred covenant. I use my energy to attract the experiences I want to manifest and God moves on my behalf to create those experiences." She was not passive in her faith. She brought her energy, her intention, her preparation — and trusted Him with the rest. I am learning to do the same.

Trust brought peace. Responsibility brought movement. Both are required. And I have found, on the other side of finally moving, that the peace and the movement are not in competition. When you are walking in alignment — when the doing matches the knowing, when the feet are moving in the direction the spirit has been pointing —

there is a particular quality of rest available to you that is not available to the woman who is bracing. It is the rest of the woman who has answered the bell. Not the absence of work. The presence of rightness.

The Flower and the Roots

What I have had to release — and this took longer than I want to admit — is the need to understand the *how.*

God's delay is not His denial. I have had to learn that more than once, because the waiting does not always feel like preparation. It feels like silence. It feels like perhaps you misread the signal, misjudged your readiness, or missed the door entirely.

But my mother knew something about growing before it shows.

She wrote, years before this chapter existed — before this book was anything more than grief and a laptop and a calling I hadn't yet agreed to answer:

> *"Before a blade of grass breaks through the ground, the roots have to be nurtured, fed and watered. The time it takes to develop the root system is time well spent, because those roots are the foundation for all future growth."*

She planted the metaphor. I grew it.

The flower does not interrogate the soil. It does not demand a timeline from the sun or insist on understanding the chemistry of its own becoming. It simply grows — in the direction it was made to grow, using what it has been given, in the season it has been placed in. The growth is happening even when nothing is visible above the surface. The roots go down before the bloom goes up. No flower has ever bloomed by worrying its way toward it.

We were not designed to know the how. We were designed to grow toward the light. The *how* belongs to God — the timing, the sequence of doors and delays He is working together behind the curtain. Our assignment is simpler and harder at the same time: stay rooted. Keep growing. Trust that the delay is not His denial — that *not yet* is not the same word as *no*.

The two-week acceleration was proof of this. I had been in the soil of that calling long before two weeks. The roots were deep before the bloom was visible. And when the door finally swung open, it was not because the delay had been a mistake. The delay had been the work.

The Reporting

I want to close where we began — at the starting line.

The grip is gone.

I am not the woman white-knuckling the familiar anymore. I am not the woman compressing her own edges into a size that fits the room she has been assigned. I am not sending the call to voicemail. I am not waiting for the conditions to feel safe enough or the doubt to clear enough or the path to be obvious enough.

I am the woman who got her laptop. Who applied for the position. Who said yes to Cynthy's Kids before she could see the how. Who, with everything the reckoning required and everything the hidden season built — agreed. Finally. Fully. Without the hedge of *eventually*.

The final 400 meters have arrived. The ground is beneath my feet and I am running.

This is the reporting for duty — a woman who, at the appointed time, stopped standing still and moved.

The breadcrumbs knew exactly where they were going. They were waiting for me to trust them enough to follow.

I do now. And the highway is already underway.

Where in your life is God ringing the bell — and what is keeping you from reporting for duty?

____

____

____

____

Not the grand, dramatic assignments. Start smaller: where have you been sending the call to voicemail? Not because you can't hear it — you can hear it — but because answering it would require you to move, and moving feels more exposed than staying.

____

____

____

Write down the two kinds of pain in your life right now. What is the discipline you are avoiding? What is the regret already accumulating? And which one are you choosing today, by the decision you are making — or not making?

____

____

____

____

Consider the difference between achievement and fulfillment in your current season. Are you building what you were made to build? Or managing something that once fit and no longer does?

____

____

____

____

Finally: what is the résumé God has been writing for you in your ordinary seasons? What have you been calling *just a job, just a season, just ordinary life* — that was actually preparation?

____

____

____

____

The flower doesn't ask how. It just grows. And so do you — whether you are paying attention to it or not. The roots are already there. What would it mean to agree with them?

____

____

____

What is your first faithful step?

____

____

____

PART IV

THE INFRASTRUCTURE OF LEGACY

"I am no longer a woman searching for a map; I am the map."

CHAPTER TEN

THE INFRASTRUCTURE OF CARE

You cannot build a legacy while running on empty.

"I had to rely on my body to tell me when to stop. But by the time I knew I was in trouble, often it was too late."

— Cynthia Davenport, The Lupus Book

The question that high-capacity people almost never ask is this: Am I tired because I am not working hard enough — or because I have been working without mercy?

There is a difference. And learning it cost me more than I expected.

I wrote in my journal one morning:

> *"Am I feeling burnt out? It feels like I'm either exhausted or sick. I can't say lazy; that just sounds ridiculous after working 6-7 days a week for the last several years."*

I was sitting with a question I did not know how to answer, because the woman I had trained myself to be did not allow for exhaustion as a valid category. She allowed for discipline, productivity, the occasional discomfort. But depletion? That wasn't in her vocabulary.

The problem was: I had clearly tried hard enough. I was working two jobs, raising two teenage daughters, managing the administrative affairs of my mother's passing. I was writing this book in the margins of nights that were already too short, and building the framework of a nonprofit at the same time. I was not failing to show up. I was showing up to everything, leaving nothing in reserve, and then waking up the next morning and doing it again.

And I was calling that *discipline*.

It wasn't discipline. It was overpayment.

The Distinction That Changes Everything

Burnout and laziness are not the same thing. I know that sounds obvious written out, but for a woman who is wired for high performance — whose identity is built on execution and reliability — the conflation of these two categories is one of the most persistent and quietly destructive errors she will ever make.

Laziness avoids responsibility. It sees the work and turns away. It will not be moved because it does not want to be moved.

Burnout carries too much responsibility. It sees the work and keeps adding to its arms even after they're full. It cannot stop because it has confused stopping with failing.

They look nothing alike from the inside. They can look almost identical from the outside. And if you are a woman of discipline — if stillness has always felt like a character flaw and rest has always felt like something you earn rather than something you need — you will consistently misread which one you are experiencing. You will try to solve your exhaustion with more structure. You will call it a motivation problem when it is actually a depletion problem.

In July of 2025, I wrote in my journal: "Am I lazy? Am I stuck? Am I procrastinating? Am I lost? Am I feeling insecure? Am I blocked? Why am I not making the necessary business moves?" I was so frustrated with myself. But the honest answer was none of those things. I was carrying too much, for too long, without a plan for replenishment.

My mother's voice arrived, as it often does, exactly when it was needed. I had heard it before. I would hear it again. But in that season of overpayment, it landed differently:

> *"You either pay now or you pay later. But everyone pays."*

I had always received that as instruction about effort — about showing up before someone makes you. What I hadn't understood is that it applies in the other direction too. You can overpay. Discipline is paying wisely. Burnout is paying too much, for too long, without replenishment. And the bill, when it finally comes due, is not one your willpower alone can overcome.

The Weight of Functioning

In the months after my mother died in May 2024, I returned to the Fifth Grade Center while continuing a second job on the weekends. I was raising two daughters who were navigating their own grief while also navigating the end of Maddie's 8th grade year and high school. I was managing the long administrative affairs of her passing. I was writing this book. I was doing all of it.

Outwardly, this looked like strength. It looked, to the people around me, like a woman who was handling things. And I was handling things. But inwardly — in the part of me that only the journal saw — it felt like lead. There were mornings when the exhaustion was a physical weight that sleep could not fix. I didn't need sleep. What I needed was permission.

Permission to be tired. Permission to put some of it down. Permission to stop solving at a pace that was costing me things I could not yet name but was definitely losing.

In November of 2025, I wrote two sentences that I have returned to many times since:

> *"It's OK to not be OK. I also believe it is not in one's best interest to stay there."*

That is the whole of it, really. Honor the low without building a home there. Acknowledge the depletion without accepting it as a permanent address. And then — when you are ready, not when someone else decides you should be — make a new choice.

I did not want to perform recovery. I wanted to actually have it. And the distinction between those two things is what this chapter is about.

Rest as Regulation

For most of my adult life, rest felt like something I had to earn. An indulgence I would allow myself once everything was caught up — knowing, of course, that everything is never caught up, and so the rest was always deferred. Always next week. Always after this particular season resolves.

What the burnout season made unavoidable is this: rest is not the opposite of discipline. It is a form of discipline. It is the discipline of taking your own biology seriously. The nervous system, when it is never allowed to downshift, eventually shuts down. That shutdown is not a character flaw. It is a biological protection. It is the body doing the only thing left available to it when you have refused to listen to every other signal it sent.

I had been refusing signals for years.

On October 19th of 2025, I wrote: "My mind and my heart understand what needs to happen, but my body is weary. I need to get to a space where my mind outweighs my body." That is the honest naming of depletion. Not a failure of character. A body keeping its record.

There were nights that season when I would sit down to write and feel a wall of resistance. The woman I had been for most of my life would have called that laziness and pushed through it. The woman I was becoming had to learn to ask a different question:

'What is this resistance protecting?'

Sometimes it was protecting me from unprocessed grief. Sometimes from sheer fatigue. Sometimes from the simple reality that the woman behind the desk had been the last person in the room to receive care — for so long that she had forgotten receiving it was an option.

Rest as regulation means understanding that your capacity is not infinite. That sustainability is not weakness. That the most disciplined choice in some seasons is not to push harder — but to pause, recalibrate, and show up tomorrow with something still in reserve.

You cannot build a legacy while running on fumes. The legacy will be built with what you actually have — not what you performed having.

She Already Knew

When the Cynthia Source File was compiled and I read her Lupus Book for the first time in its entirety, I had to stop.

My mother had already written this chapter.

Decades before I sat down to name the infrastructure of care — before I could articulate burnout versus discipline, before I understood rest as regulation rather than reward — she had documented all of it. She had lived it. She had survived it.

She wrote, in Chapter Three of her Lupus Book:

> *"In the beginning of my lupus journey, I had no idea how close I was to a meltdown on any given day. I had to rely on my body to tell me when to stop. But by the time I knew I was in trouble, often it was too late. Learning to see the signs of fatigue earlier took a few years for me to master. I learned to break big tasks into smaller steps to conserve my energy. Pacing myself became a way of life."*

She was not writing about failure. She was writing about hard-won wisdom. She had been one of those high-capacity people too — the woman who could run from Illinois Bell to law school, who could drive Uber and Lyft on a disability check, who could hold a household and raise children and still show up for her people. And then lupus introduced her to a body that could no longer push through on will alone. And she listened. She learned. She paced.

She went on to write:

> *"I manage stress by walking, reading, burning scented candles, and laughing a lot. Turns out being happy is good medicine too!"*

That is pure Cynthia. Upbeat and practical even inside conditions that would have broken most people. She did not romanticize the limitation. She built a system around it. She curated her environment — the candles, the peaceful home, the toxic people firmly on the outside. She called it her haven. She made it deliberately and she protected it.

She had already written this chapter. I just didn't know it yet. The Primary Architect built this into the blueprint before I ever knew I would need it.

Mother and daughter. The same truth. Arrived at differently. Decades apart. We were just listening to the same God.

Curated Input as Daily Infrastructure

The stewardship of the mind is not a vague spiritual concept. It is a daily operational decision. What you allow your eyes, ears, and hours to consume is an infrastructure choice. And in this season, I had to make some changes.

In January of 2025, I wrote: "So now that I've put down watching 5-6 hours every night of MSNBC news programs and significantly reduced Facebook and Instagram scrolling, I can use that time minding my business."

That phrase —

minding my business — is doing real work. It means: my business. My book. My financial literacy. My journal. My becoming. Those hours were not empty before; they were full of noise that belonged to everyone else's emergency. And they were consuming time that belonged to mine.

On August 11th of 2025, I wrote a set of daily questions I began asking myself:

> *Am I willing to read for at least 30 minutes a day?*
>
> *Am I willing to get up an hour earlier or go for a walk after work, three to five days a week?*
>
> *Am I willing to put time into my personal development that will change my future financial outlook?*
>
> *Am I willing to do the work?*

And then, this part: "Somedays the answer might be no to one or more of these questions. Each day ask yourself these questions. Keep striving until your answer is a resounding YES! Don't get down on yourself about the choice of NO — just make a new choice the next day. Or the next day after that."

That is infrastructure thinking. It is not a single heroic effort or a permanent white-knuckling effort. It is a daily decision, made again each morning, about what you will allow into the space that belongs to your future.

My mother managed stress by walking and reading and burning scented candles and laughing a lot. I began managing mine by protecting the morning hours and choosing what my mind consumed before the world got loud. Different forms. Same principle. The vessel must be stewarded, or it cannot hold what it is meant to carry.

Strength Without Hardness

My brain had been wired to believe that strength required tightening.

After the car accident in 2002, I braced. After my mother died, I functioned. At work, I executed. At home, I managed. In every room that needed steadiness, I provided it. To me, strength looked like competence. Competence looked like control. And control felt far safer than anything that resembled softness.

What I did not yet understand is that control was never real to begin with. The illusion of it was real — the tightening, the vigilance, the careful management of every outcome within reach. But control itself? It was the story I told myself to make the bracing feel like a choice. The asphalt in New Mexico reminded me of that in 2002. Grief reminded me again in 2024. You are not in control. You never were. What you have is how you respond.

I had absorbed, somewhere along the way, the whispered binary that culture offers women: be ambitious or be tender. Be capable or be cared for. Be strong or be soft. Choose one. And because strength had been the tool that kept me upright through some very steep terrain, I had built the entire interior architecture of my life around it.

What I had not understood — what this season finally made me see — is that there is a difference between strength and armor. Armor keeps you safe. But armor also keeps you inaccessible. You cannot be truly known inside armor. You cannot truly receive inside it. And you cannot build a lasting legacy while gripping the familiar with both hands, because both hands are busy holding on.

When Dr. Pam named the ice block in January of 2026, she was naming more than a physical injury. She was naming the place where my body had been holding the cost of decades of armor. The thaw was about more than the spine. It was permission — permission to lead without overcompensating, to be ambitious without apologizing, to show up powerful in the world without needing to be impenetrable at home.

Strength without hardness is not weakness. It is strength without fear. It is knowing you are capable — and not needing to prove it with your posture.

What I Had to Forgive Myself For

In Chapter Eight, I sat with the ledger and opened it. I named the things that were mine to own. But there is a specific entry that belongs here — because it is the one most relevant to how a high-capacity woman runs herself into the ground while calling it faithfulness.

I had to forgive myself for the years I mistook bracing for strength.

The forgiveness was quiet and firm. An acknowledgment, long overdue, that I had been operating with a definition of strength that was not serving me and was not serving the people I loved. The woman who kept going when she should have rested — who filed the paperwork and managed the feelings and held the room together and never let anyone see the cost — was not wrong for doing those things. She did what the season required. She did what she had to do, in the moment she found herself in.

But she does not have to keep doing it that way.

Forgiveness, in this context, means releasing the pattern and looking at the woman who confused endurance with virtue and saying...

> *"I understand why you built yourself this way. You were surviving. And what you built held. And it is time, now, to build something different."*

The personal responsibility of this chapter is not just about knowing when you've hit your limit. It is about giving yourself permission to honor that limit without shame. Because you cannot pour from a vessel you have drained and refused to refill. And you cannot offer your husband and daughters — or the people Cynthy's Kids will serve — your very best, while spending yourself trying to prove you are enough.

You already are enough. That is not the question. The question is whether you are willing to protect what you are, so it can be given fully and sustainably, for as long as you are called to give it.

The Oxygen Mask Is Not a Metaphor for Selfishness

We have already established the instruction: put your own mask on first. I said it in an earlier chapter for a reason — because it was the principle my mother modeled in her dying, and because grief forced me to reckon with how consistently I had applied it to others and withheld it from myself.

But in the weeks after my medical procedure in February of 2025, the instruction became personal in a way I had not anticipated.

My mother was gone. The woman who would have been there to hold my hand, to help around the house, to simply sit in the room with me the way mothers do — she was not there. And in her absence, something became undeniable: I had been leaning on her as a safety net in ways I had not fully named while she was alive. When the safety net was gone, I had to learn, for perhaps the first time in my adult life, to fully receive care — from my husband, from my daughters, from God — without immediately calculating when I could get back to giving it.

I wrote on that birthday: "Nothing compares to a momma." And that is simply true. But the season after her passing was the one that finally asked me to tend to myself with the seriousness she would have wanted me to. She spent the last years of her life building a haven — candles, warmth, peace, laughter — because she had learned what happens when the body is not given what it needs. I am her daughter. The lesson was always meant to reach me too.

Stewardship is not just about the vision. It is about the vessel.

Cynthy's Kids was born from twenty years of accumulated preparation. But the woman who is building it has to still be standing when the building matters most. She has to still have something left to give when her husband and daughters need her. She has to be the woman who puts on the oxygen mask — not because she is selfish, but because she understands that her presence, her health, and her capacity are not incidental to the legacy. They are the infrastructure of it.

Knowing your limits is stewardship, not weakness. Taking rest seriously is not laziness. It is the discipline of a woman who intends to still be building ten years from now.

The Integrated Woman

The woman who survived the car accident in 2002. The administrator who built systems for twenty years in buildings that were not hers to lead. The daughter who held her mother's hand in the hospice room and then picked herself up and kept going. The founder sitting down to draft the bylaws of a nonprofit at midnight while the house is quiet.

These are not different women. They are not fragmented chapters of a life that never quite cohered. They are one woman — arriving at herself slowly, imperfectly, and finally.

Little Liz — the four-year-old who learned to brace in the courthouse, who perfected the art of composed survival, who carried a weight that was never hers to carry and did it quietly for four decades — she has finally been given permission to stand down. The adult woman has stepped forward to lead. The pain may still be present. The work is far from done. But she is leading anyway.

And she does not need to be braced to do it.

She is not white-knuckling the familiar anymore. She is not performing strength for the benefit of the room. She has done the work. She has opened the ledger. She has thawed what was frozen, released what needed releasing, and owned what needed owning.

And now she is building.

What my daughters will see is not a woman who had it all together. I am a woman who chose, repeatedly and under conditions that could have justified otherwise, to keep going with honesty rather than performance. They will see a woman who rested when rest was required and moved when movement was required and knew the difference — eventually. They will see a woman who carried her mother's memory not as a weight, but as a compass.

My mother managed what she was given with grace, humor, candles, and laughter. She paced herself. She built a haven. She decided she was going to live until she died — and she did.

I am her daughter. I carry that forward.

"Still together. Just a little different."

The ice block is thawing. The courthouse is behind her. The legacy is ahead.

She is building. And she is not building alone.

Are you disciplined or depleted right now?

Those are different things. Sit with the question. Don't rush past it.

Discipline chooses discomfort intentionally, with a purpose. Depletion absorbs it indiscriminately, until the body makes the decision the mind refused to make.

Where in your life have you been calling depletion discipline? What have you been carrying that has your name on it but was never supposed to be a permanent load?

____

____

____

And this: What does responsible rest look like for you in this specific season? Not rest as an abstract concept — the actual form it would take. Tomorrow. This week. Name it.

____

____

____

Write it down. And then — this is the accountability part — tell someone.

____

____

____

You cannot build what you are called to build while running on survival mode. The legacy requires the vessel. Steward them both.

My mother already showed you how. She paced herself. She protected her haven. She kept laughing.

CYNTHY'S KIDS, INC.

Legacy is not a monument you leave behind. It is something you build, every day you are still here to build it.

Writing This Book Saved My Sanity

Writing this book saved my sanity.

I have a picture in my mind — an image I came across somewhere in the middle of all of this — of a woman whose face is split down the center. One side of her is silent and deeply sad. The other side of her is screaming. I could relate to both halves.

There was a version of me, in the months after my mother died, who was coasting — showing up to everything except inside her own purpose. Still showing up to work, still caring for my husband and daughters, still managing the things that needed managing. But underneath the functioning there was a fracture. I was having a hard time reconciling the woman my mother raised me to be and the woman

I was becoming — a woman being slowly overwhelmed by grief, by exhaustion, by the particular loneliness of being strong in every room and unraveling in none of them.

I was in therapy. I was still writing in my Notes app. But I did not have purpose. I was just barely coasting and growing more frustrated with myself every passing day. There had to be an off-ramp somewhere. The way I was living was not sustainable. I knew that.

And then I found out something that grief had been doing to me without my realizing it.

Grief, like many other types of trauma, can have a way of cocooning you in your own world. You can get so wrapped up in your own pain that you forget to look up and out to see that others may be hurting, too.

The moment I looked up was the moment Cynthy's Kids became more than an idea.

I am not sure I could have built this while still cocooned. I am not sure the vision could have crystallized until I was grieving with my eyes open instead of just surviving with them closed. This book was the thing that cracked the cocoon. And what emerged when it finally opened was not just a healed woman. It was a woman with a mission.

Legacy Is a Verb

I used to think of legacy the way most people do — as something that arrives after you are gone. A name on a headstone. A photograph in a frame. A story someone tells at a funeral about the kind of person you were.

I did not understand, until my mother died, that I had been waiting for legacy to happen to me. That I had confused the noun with the verb.

In January of 2026, I was in my chair, phone in hand, typing into the Notes app where I had been chronicling this entire journey. The vision poured out faster than my thumbs could keep up:

> *Birth of a dream — Cynthy's Kids — Financial Empowerment and Community Center… offers math, science, tutoring, financial literacy classes at different age groups… stock training… business ownership classes… real estate training… retirement planning… provide a place for authors to come in for book signings.*

I was sitting with a future in my chest that did not yet have a name. The vision poured out in the urgent shorthand of a woman who understood that if she did not capture it immediately, it might recede back into the place where dreams wait until you are brave enough to call them assignments.

That was the moment legacy stopped being a noun for me.

My mother did not leave a legacy by standing still. She left one by moving — by choosing, every single day of a life complicated by illness and limited resources and a body that was working against her, to be present and intentional and forward-facing. I have written in these pages about what she kept on her refrigerator. I return to it here because this is the chapter that mantra was always pointing toward:

> *"In the end, it is good. If it is not good, it is not the end."*

She repeated it until it was no longer a coping mechanism. It became a theology. She passed that theology to me slowly, the way roots grow — morning after morning of watching her choose forward over frozen.

That is legacy as a verb. That is what I am inheriting. That is what I am building.

The Why Behind the Mission

The story behind this nonprofit begins in a harder place than a dream. It begins in watching my mother navigate a system that was never built for her. My mother was a smart woman. She graduated from Roosevelt University in 1992 with a Bachelor of Arts in Political Science after leaving a stable job at Illinois Bell to go back to school as a single mother with two children. She did this while battling a body that was beginning to turn against her. Her plan, after graduation, was law school.

Then came the lupus diagnosis in 1994, and congestive heart failure. The law school dream did not die easily — she fought for it — but eventually her body made the decision her will refused to. The career she had mapped out became unavailable to her. She had to pivot, over and over, for decades.

In the years that followed, she drove for Uber and Lyft on a disability check — her way of surviving a system that penalizes you for earning too much. If you make above a certain threshold, the check gets cut. So, she did what she could, as long as she could, within the constraints of a system that treated her survival as a ceiling rather than a floor.

I wrote about this in my notes: *"She could only make so much money before it would start affecting her disability check. You can't build wealth that way, much less generational wealth."*

She left a modest amount when she died. The systems she navigated had a ceiling built into them, and no one had ever handed her a blueprint for getting around it. There was no community table, no financial literacy program, no place that met her where she was and showed her a path forward while she was young enough to walk it.

In January of 2026, my husband and I sat across from a financial advisor and told him we wanted to establish a trust. He told us it was a waste of time and money.

I knew immediately we would not be hiring him.

What I wrote about it in my Notes app captures exactly why: he could only see DuJuan and me as the people we are today. He was not interested in seeing us the way we see ourselves in the future. We are planning based on where we are headed, not where we are currently.

That is what Cynthy's Kids is. It is a table built for people who have been told their future is a waste of time and money. It is a structure built because I watched my mother drive Lyft on a disability check and decided that story would end differently for the next generation.

That is the pain that built the mission. That is the why cemented into my backbone.

Little Liz Stands Down

Before I could build anything, I had to put something down.

I have written in these pages about the four-year-old girl I call Little Liz — the child who stood in a Chicago courthouse in 1982 and was asked to perform an adult's surgery on herself. Choose which parent. Choose which half of your heart. Report your answer to a stranger in a robe.

She did what children do when the world asks too much of them: she braced. She went still. She learned that survival looked like composure, that safety looked like not needing anything from anyone, that being strong meant being the one who did not cry in the courthouse.

For forty-three years, she carried that posture with her into every room she entered.

I see her clearly now. She is sitting on a cold wooden bench, her feet not quite reaching the floor, swallowed by a room that feels like a mountain range. She is wearing her best dress. She is holding very, very still. She has been told, in ways that no adult actually said out loud but that she understood perfectly, that the right answer matters.

She was not responsible. She was four years old. She was just a child, standing in a room full of adult decisions, doing the only thing she knew how to do.

What I had to do, to build Cynthy's Kids, was walk back into that courthouse — in the way healing requires — and speak the verdict that no one ever gave her.

It was not your fault. I said it slowly, the way you say something to someone who has been waiting a long time to hear it. *You were not the judge. You were not the cause. You were just a child. And you did not deserve to carry this.*

And then I had to forgive.

This kind of forgiveness is bone-deep and structural — it clears the ground so something new can be built on it. The kind where you look at everyone who was present when the wound happened — people who were imperfect, navigating their own broken places, doing the best they could in a season they were not equipped for — and you make a decision.

An earlier chapter of this book holds a truth my father shared with me that I have been carrying ever since: as parents, we do the best we can, in the season we are in, with the resources we have available. I bring it here because it applies not just to the parents in the room, but to the child. Little Liz did the best she could, in the season she was in, with the resources she had. Which were none. She had a dress and her stillness and the hope that being good enough would keep the world from falling any further apart.

Forgiveness, I have learned, is not a gift for the person who wounded you. It is the act of releasing yourself from the obligation to keep carrying what they did. You are deciding — with full knowledge of what it cost you — that you are no longer willing to let it set the ceiling on what you build.

Little Liz waited forty-three years for permission to leave that courthouse. I am giving it to her now.

You are free. The verdict is in. You were innocent. And it is time to build.

I watch her, in my mind, as the invisible shield she has carried since 1982 finally hits the floor. And in the quiet that follows, she looks up. Not at the courtroom doors behind her. At the stars ahead.

She is not a lost child anymore. She is the foundation upon which I am building everything else.

Honoring the Architect

Cynthy's Kids is named for a woman who understood, decades before I did, that everything is preparation. In the letter to her grand-daughters, she wrote that alchemy and serendipity are like breadcrumbs that help lead you toward your destiny one step at a time — the very metaphor at the center of this book, coined by her before I wrote a single word of it. The title was always hers.

She carried her faith the way people carry something they have tested and found true — with the quiet certainty of a woman who had watched it hold under pressure. She had been a minister's wife. She had sat in church pews and taught Sunday school and absorbed scripture into her bones. Over time, her faith evolved beyond any institution into something larger and more personal — a theology of resilience, a conviction that the worst things do not get the final word.

She proved it. She navigated thirty years of lupus and congestive heart failure with what her doctors called, more than once, inexplicable grace. She lived by a sentence she wrote in her journal: *"On paper my condition was grave, but in person I was upbeat and positive."*

She decided, somewhere in the middle of an impossible body, a derailed career, and a life that had asked far too much of her, that she was going to live until she died. And she did. Fully. On her own terms.

Cynthy's Kids is named for the theology she lived. The grief is woven into every page of this book, but the name belongs to something larger — the evidence she left that grit, faith, and tenacity are possible under impossible conditions.

I could feel her as the vision formed. The way you feel a strong wind when you have just opened a door — you do not see it, but you know without question it is there.

Still together. Just a little different.

This Is Being Orchestrated

I have been recording voice notes throughout the writing of this book. Thoughts that arrived too fast for the Notes app, revelations I needed to say out loud to hear them properly. And in February of 2026, I said this:

> *This is being orchestrated. It is being completely assembled in the spirit realm, and then it is being manifested in the physical world.*

I believed it when I said it. I still believe it now.

I did not build Cynthy's Kids. I agreed with what was already being built. My twenty years of administrative labor — the spreadsheets, the handbooks, the Standard Operating Procedures, the programs built from scratch at City Garden and maintained at the Fifth Grade Center — none of that was random. None of it was wasting time. It was preparation. The hands that would draft the bylaws for this nonprofit had spent two decades learning how to draft things that hold.

God told me: I've been preparing you for this for over twenty years. You just didn't know it. You thought you were aimlessly wandering from spot to spot. You weren't. Every step was a brick.

The nonprofit did not appear in a vacuum. It formed in the frustration of watching my mother navigate systems designed to keep people like her from accumulating anything. It formed in the recognition that financial illiteracy is not a character flaw — it is a systemic vulnerability, and it is entirely addressable. It formed because I realized that children who look like my daughters, Elise and Madelyn, deserve infrastructure, not just encouragement. Every step I had taken for twenty years was already part of the blueprint — I just could not see the drawing yet.

February 17, 2026

The letter arrived on a Tuesday.

There was no ceremony. No camera. No gathering. Just me, sitting in my chair in my office, reading the official letter of incorporation for Cynthy's Kids, Inc., dated February 17, 2026, still warm from the printer.

I read it twice. And then I stayed there because something in me needed to be still for a moment. Something that had been running for a very long time needed to pause and acknowledge that the thing we had been moving toward had arrived.

I cried. Happy tears. They were the tears of a woman who had arrived somewhere she was told, in a hundred quiet ways by a hundred quiet fears, she might not be allowed to go.

I thought about my mother.

I thought about Illinois Bell and the law school that never happened. About the Uber and the Lyft and the disability ceiling. About the modest amount she left and the financial advisor who told us a trust was a waste of time. About the courthouse in 1982 and the asphalt in New Mexico in 2002 and the hospice bedroom in May 2024. About every spreadsheet I dismissed as ordinary while God was filing it under formation.

All of it had been leading here.

I felt my mother's smile in the way you feel something that is real and present and just beyond what your eyes can reach. I felt it the way I would have felt it if I could have called her:

Mom. We did it. The thing you always said I was capable of. The thing I kept sending to voicemail. It's here. It's real. It has a name.

| *"In the end, it is good. If it is not good, it is not the end."*

This is the good. This is the end she was always pointing me toward.

The Blueprint of Cynthy's Kids

Cynthy's Kids, Inc. is an institution rooted in a blueprint my mother spent her whole life drawing. And the blueprint has specific, structural plans.

Our first and most immediate initiative is scholarships — providing financial support to students seeking to advance in higher education who would not otherwise have access to what they need to get there. We are already planning to celebrate our first scholarship recipients at our inaugural awards banquet in Spring 2027. We are working toward it now.

Within the next two to five years, we will expand into tutoring and financial literacy programming — built around the conviction that what gets passed down in a family shapes a child's life long before she ever sets foot in a classroom. The relationship with money, the understanding of how it moves and grows, the knowledge that you can sign your own check rather than wait for someone else to sign it — these are inheritances, and every child deserves them.

The long-term vision — the ten-year goal I carry in my chest like a compass — is a physical Community and Empowerment Center, a building with Cynthy's name on the door. A beacon that offers tutoring in math, science, typing, and cursive writing. Financial literacy classes tailored to every age group. Stock market education. Business ownership and real estate fundamentals. Retirement planning. A space where authors come in for book signings and community members gather to learn what wealthy people were taught early and the rest of us are learning late.

This is a destination with a timeline and a name. And I am building toward it with a discipline that twenty years of administrative work built into my hands before I knew what they were building toward.

Changing the Narrative of Wealth

I want to change the way our community talks about money. And I want to start with the children.

Why are we waiting until our kids are teenagers to begin the conversation about ownership and investing, if then? In my vision, a kindergartner is learning the basics of ownership and numbers through Monopoly Junior. A middle schooler is reading a basic financial report and opening her first brokerage account with money she earned through a fundraiser — learning that money can work for her before she is old enough to need it to.

By high school, our students would understand how compounding works. They would understand the stock market. They would understand options as young people who have been equipped with the literacy to make informed decisions about their own futures. They would be taught to leverage their minds rather than only their physical labor. They would be learning what it means to sign their own checks rather than waiting for someone else's signature to authorize their life.

My mother worked for decades. She was smart, tenacious, and faithful. She also drove for Uber and Lyft on a disability check because the systems around her were built to keep that check small. She had dreams and plans and a body that eventually could not keep up with either — and a system that had no interest in bridging the gap.

I am building what she did not have access to. I am building it for the children who look like my daughters. Because every child deserves infrastructure, not just inspiration. Because inspiration without structure leaves people motivated and unprepared. Because the most loving thing you can do for a child is give them the tools to build their own life.

This is what my mother planted. I am cultivating the harvest.

The Final Act of Stewardship

This chapter is about personal responsibility in its final form — the expression of it that comes after all the inner work has been done and the only question left is what you will build with it.

I sent the call to voicemail. More than once. I told myself I was not ready, not qualified, not the kind of person who builds foundations and names them after her mother. I confused humility with smallness. I confused readiness with perfection. I waited.

On my forty-seventh birthday — February 27, 2025 — I wrote: I feel like my why is being cemented firmly into my backbone.

That sentence told me the waiting was almost over.

The final act of stewardship is building something that outlives you. It is taking everything formed in the hidden seasons — every spreadsheet, every SOP, every moment of administrative discipline you dismissed as ordinary while God filed it under formation — and putting it in service of something that will still be standing after you are gone. That is the response to everything He has been building in you. Not gratitude alone. Activation.

You cannot build a legacy with a hand still pointing at someone else. And you cannot build a legacy while hiding from the size of your own calling.

Cynthy's Kids is the evidence that I stopped hiding. It is the proof that I picked up the call.

The Final 400 Meters

I return often to the track.

I have been running this race for a long time. There have been miles where the terrain was brutal and the finish line was nowhere in sight. There have been miles where I ran beautifully, in rhythm, with the confidence of a woman who trusts her training. And there have been miles — long ones — where I was running on fumes, bracing against the next impact, telling myself that survival was the same thing as progress.

It is not. But I understand now why I confused them.

The final 400 meters are different. The exhaustion is real. The weight of everything you have carried to get here is real. But the finish line is visible. And something changes when you can see it.

You do not slow down. You sprint.

I had already written the declaration months before the incorporation letter arrived. In an earlier chapter I put those words down in full — the urgency, the sprint, the command to finish strong — because that is where they first landed, in September of 2025, before there was anything yet to show for them. The faith came before the evidence. That is the whole theology of this book. What I know now, standing on this side of February 17, 2026, is that the sprint I declared that September was not the finish. It was just finding its legs.

The call is no longer on voicemail. I have answered it. I am reporting for duty.

My mother ran her portion of this race. She handed me the baton covered in her faith and her grit and her thirty years of surviving what should have stopped her. She is in the stands now. I can feel her watching. I am not running away from grief. I am running toward the thing she always believed I was capable of building.

Still together. Just a little different.

The Extension of the Divine

My love and trust in God are no longer a concept I visit on Sundays. It is the atmosphere in which I reside. I do not walk beside Him. I do not merely follow Him. I reside in Him, and He resides in me. That sacred indwelling is the source of my actual confidence — the quiet, settled kind that belongs to a woman who knows Whose she is.

He was with me in the Chicago courthouse in 1982. He was with me on the New Mexico asphalt in 2002. He was in the hospice bedroom in May 2024. He was in every spreadsheet. Every SOP. Every "Ms. Liz" moment with a student who needed a boundary to feel safe.

He was building a curriculum out of everything I thought I was just doing. My readiness belongs entirely to His relentless preparation — the kind that takes the long view, that uses the detour instead of avoiding it, that makes the hidden season count even when no one is watching. Especially when no one is watching.

I am no longer Little Liz standing in the shadows of the courthouse, waiting for a verdict that was never mine to receive. I am the woman who sat in her office on a Tuesday in February and read an incorporation letter with tears running down her face.

I am the woman who answers the call.

I am an extension of the Divine. And I have work to do.

Final Benediction: The Breadcrumbs Were Always There

This is where I was going.

All of it — the courthouse and the asphalt and the hospice bedroom and the twenty years of administrative labor and the ice block in my back and the grief that felt like it would obliterate me and the Notes app entries at midnight and the moments of terrible stillness and the moments of unmistakable clarity — all of it was pointing here.

Here as in: the life of a woman who stopped bracing and started building. Who stopped sending the call to voicemail and started picking up. Who took the breadcrumbs she was given — the small ones, the quiet ones, the ones she almost missed because she was looking for something bigger and more obvious — and followed them all the way home.

The breadcrumbs were always there.

Nothing was wasted. Not the courthouse. Not the asphalt. Not the devastated child inside her who had been waiting four decades to be told she could finally stand down. Not the grief. Not the ice. Not the hidden season that felt like obscurity and was actually formation.

God does not waste what He builds. He just builds slowly, and mostly in the dark, and usually in ways that look nothing like the thing being built until you are far enough along the path to turn around and see the trail.

I have turned around. I can see it now.

And my mother — the woman who coined the breadcrumb metaphor in a letter to her granddaughters ten years before this book existed — she saw it before I did.

There are children I have not yet met who are already being prepared for what Cynthy's Kids will offer them. There are families navigating right now what I navigated — the impossible arithmetic of caring for an aging parent while raising children and holding a career together — who need to know that someone built a structure for people like them. There is a building, somewhere in this city, that will one day have Cynthy's name on it.

I am not running away from my mother's death. I am running toward everything she always believed I was.

In the end, it is good. If it is not good, it is not the end.

The end is good. The work continues. And I am finally — fully, freely, and without apology — reporting for duty.

The grief that felt like it would consume you was also the thing that cracked the cocoon open. Sit with that. Because it means your pain was never just your pain. It was always preparation for something larger than yourself. What legacy are you being called to build? Not the one that sounds responsible or manageable. The real one — the one pressing against the inside of your chest for longer than you want to admit. What breadcrumbs has God already placed in your path that you have been dismissing as ordinary? What hidden season that felt like waiting was actually formation? Who is the Little Liz in your story — the part of you that learned to brace in a moment that asked too much of a child? What would it mean to forgive what built that wound — not for their sake, but for yours? What becomes possible when that hand finally unclenches? And this: what is one faithful step you can take this week toward the thing you are being called to build? Not the whole plan. Not the bylaws or the ten-year vision. Just the next breadcrumb. Follow it. The trail was laid for you long before you were ready to walk it. And you are ready now.

REFLECTION & INTEGRATION SUITE

THE BREADCRUMB TIMELINE

*Mapping the path God has already been
forming in your life*

When we look forward, life often feels uncertain and uncharted. But when we look backward — when we pause long enough to survey the terrain we've already crossed — patterns begin to emerge. Moments that felt random reveal themselves as deliberate. Seasons that felt like setbacks reveal themselves as preparation. This is the nature of breadcrumbs: they only make sense when you turn around and look.

Take your time with this exercise. You have earned the right to see your own story clearly.

Impact Moments

Events that changed your direction, your perspective, or your understanding of who you are.

Examples: loss · illness · accidents · major disappointments · unexpected changes

Write your moments here:

____

____

____

____

____

____

____

____

____

Preparation Seasons

Times when you were learning, growing, or building skills — even when you didn't recognize it as preparation.

Examples: education · parenting seasons · difficult jobs · caregiving · seasons of waiting

____

____

____

____

____

____

____

Pivot Points

Moments when a decision — yours or someone else's — redirected the course of your life.

Examples: saying yes to something new · leaving something behind · stepping into leadership · choosing obedience

---

Current Breadcrumb

What might God be inviting you toward right now?

Your Next Faithful Step

What is one step of obedience you can take this week?

THE BREADCRUMB MAP

Every life leaves a trail — take time to trace yours

Every life leaves a trail of breadcrumbs. When you step back and observe your story with compassion and curiosity, you begin to see that the moments which once felt random were actually preparation. God wastes nothing — not the loss, not the waiting, not the quiet years of hidden labor.

Take time to identify your own breadcrumbs. There is no right answer. There is only your truth.

My Earliest Formation

What shaped you before you had words for it? What did your earliest years teach you about safety, about faith, about who you were allowed to become?

____

____

____

____

____

____

The Hard Season That Changed Me

What was the hardest thing you've lived through? What did it take from you — and what did it, quietly, give you?

The Lessons I Carry Forward

What do you know now that you didn't know before? What is the lesson embedded in the experience?

The Calling I Sense Emerging

What stirs in you when you read about legacy, about purpose, about being a divine extension? What is the thing you keep returning to?

7 DAYS OF FOLLOWING THE BREADCRUMBS

One scripture. One reflection. One step of obedience.

Use the next seven days to reflect on how God has been moving in your life. This is not a performance. There is no grade. This is simply seven days of paying attention — to what God has already done, and to what He may be preparing you for next.

Day 1: Remember the Impact

"And we know that in all things God works for the good of those who love him, who have been called according to his purpose."
— Romans 8:28 (NIV)

Context

The Apostle Paul wrote this letter to believers in Rome who were experiencing suffering, persecution, and uncertainty. In this chapter, Paul is explaining that life in the Spirit does not remove hardship—but it reframes it. This verse is not saying everything is good; it is saying God is actively working through everything—even pain—to accomplish His purpose in those who trust Him.

Reflection

If I'm honest, I spent years trying to outrun my impact moments rather than learn from them. The car accident. The courthouse at four years old. The hospice room in May 2024. Each one felt like a full stop. But God doesn't write in full stops. He writes in chapters. The moment that changed you? It was the beginning of the chapter — not the end of the book. Even the hardest moments in our lives can become part of God's formation process. Impact does not end your story. It often begins a deeper one.

My mother loved Mary Stevenson's poem "Footprints in the Sand." In it, a person looks back at the path of their life and notices that in the hardest seasons — the seasons of deepest pain and loss — there is only one set of footprints in the sand. They ask God why He abandoned them in those moments. And God answers: those were not the seasons I left you. Those were the seasons I carried you. That poem lived on my mother's heart for a reason. Because the breadcrumbs were there in the darkest chapters too — even when she couldn't see them. Even when I couldn't see them. God was not absent. He was carrying us both.

Question

What moment in your life changed how you see the world? What shaped you the most?

Prayer

God, help me see how You have been present even in the hardest seasons of my life. Teach me to find Your fingerprints in the places I've been most afraid to look. Amen.

Day 2: Nothing Was Wasted

"I will repay you for the years the locusts have eaten…"
— *Joel 2:25 (NIV)*

Context

The prophet Joel is speaking to Israel after a devastating locust plague that destroyed their crops and livelihood. This wasn't just economic loss—it was emotional, spiritual, and generational impact. God promises restoration—not just of resources, but of time, loss, and what felt irrecoverable.

Reflection

I used to grieve the years I spent in administrative work before my calling crystallized. I thought I was behind schedule. What I didn't know is that God's schedule is written in invisible ink — it only becomes legible in hindsight. The seasons you called wasted? They were workshops. The jobs that felt like detours? They were the curriculum. You just didn't have the syllabus yet. God often restores what we thought was permanently lost — and He returns it transformed.

Question

Where have you seen restoration in your life? What did you think was lost that God returned — different, but whole?

____

____

____

____

____

____

____

Prayer

Lord, open my eyes to the work You have been doing behind the scenes. Thank You for redeeming the seasons I called wasted. Amen.

Day 3: Discipline

"No discipline seems pleasant at the time, but painful. Later on, however, it produces a harvest of righteousness and peace for those who have been trained by it." — Hebrews 12:11 (NIV)

Context

The writer of Hebrews is encouraging believers who are growing weary under pressure. He compares life's challenges and discipline to a loving father training a child—not punishment, but formation. Discipline is evidence of care, not rejection.

Reflection

My mother had a saying I didn't fully appreciate until I was grown: "You either pay now or you pay later. But everyone pays." She was talking about discipline. The price of discipline is paid in the quiet, before anyone is watching. The price of regret is paid in public, after it's too late to change anything. Discipline feels uncomfortable in the moment. But regret costs more than discipline ever will — and it lingers longer. The choice is always ours, and it is always ours to make again, today.

Question

What area of your life needs consistent discipline? What could change
in the next year if you practiced it faithfully?

____

____

____

____

____

____

____

____

Prayer

God, give me the strength to choose growth today — even when it's
uncomfortable, even when no one is watching. Amen.

Day 4: Relationships

_"There is a time for everything, and a season for every activity under
the heavens." — Ecclesiastes 3:1 (NIV)_

Context

Written by Solomon, this passage reflects on the rhythms of life—birth, death, planting, uprooting. It acknowledges that life is not linear or controllable. Instead, it unfolds in divinely appointed seasons. Wisdom is not forcing the wrong season; it is recognizing the one you are in.

Reflection

Some of the hardest spiritual work I've done has been around releasing relationships I thought were permanent. What I've come to understand is that people come into our lives for a reason, a season, or a lifetime — and confusing the category is where so much heartbreak lives. Releasing a seasonal relationship is not failure. It is discernment. Some relationships are meant for a season. You are not required to be bitter about their ending. But you are permitted to grieve. And then, with God's help, you are called to release with grace.

Question

Who might God be asking you to release — gently, lovingly, and without bitterness?

____

____

____

____

____

Prayer

Help me trust You with every relationship in my life — the ones I'm holding and the ones I need to lay down. Amen.

Day 5: Strength and Softness

"She is clothed with strength and dignity; she can laugh at the days to come." — Proverbs 31:25 (NIV)

Context

This is part of a larger description of a woman of wisdom, character, and stewardship. Her strength is not loud—it is rooted in confidence, preparation, and trust in God, which allows her to face the future without fear.

Reflection

I spent a long time believing that softness was something I couldn't afford. That the world required armor, and that tenderness was a liability.

What I've learned — in a chiropractor's office, in a hospice room, and in a hundred quiet mornings with God — is that the strongest thing I own is my tenderness. Armor keeps things out. Tenderness lets the right things in. You do not have to sacrifice your gentleness to walk in your authority. The two were always meant to travel together.

Question

Where do you need to ask for support instead of carrying everything alone? What would it feel like to lay the armor down?

Prayer

Teach me to walk in both courage and tenderness — to be strong without being hard, and soft without being small. Amen.

Day 6: Divine Timing

"For the revelation awaits an appointed time; it speaks of the end and will not prove false. Though it linger, wait for it; it will certainly come and will not delay." — Habakkuk 2:3 (NIV)

Context

The prophet Habakkuk is questioning God about injustice and delay. God responds by telling him that the vision will come—but not on human timing. Waiting is not denial; it is part of fulfillment.

Reflection

God's delay is not His denial. I know this now in my bones — but there was a season when His silence felt like abandonment, when the waiting felt like punishment for something I couldn't name. What I didn't know then is that the delay was the preparation. What was growing in me during the hidden season was exactly what the purpose required. The flower doesn't ask why it's still in the ground. It just grows. It just becomes. God's timing often only becomes clear in hindsight — and what looked like delay was simply preparation in motion.

Question

What waiting season may have been preparation in disguise? What grew in you during the waiting that you didn't recognize until later?

____

____

____

____

____

____

____

____

Prayer

Help me trust Your timing over my urgency. Remind me that what I'm waiting for is also waiting to be ready. Amen.

Day 7: The Next Breadcrumb

"Your word is a lamp for my feet, a light on my path."
— Psalm 119:105 (NIV)

Context

Psalm 119 is the longest chapter in the Bible, and it focuses entirely on the value of God's Word. This verse emphasizes that God does not always reveal the entire path—He provides just enough light for the next step. Obedience to what is already illuminated is what keeps the light moving forward.

Reflection

You have arrived at Day 7. Look at what you've survived to get here — not just this week, but your entire life. Every impact moment, every hidden season, every pivot point that redirected you toward something you couldn't yet see. God did not bring you through all of that to drop you at the edge of your purpose. He brought you through it to your purpose. God rarely reveals the entire path — only the next step. The next breadcrumb is already in front of you. The question is simply whether you're ready to take the step.

Question

What breadcrumb is in front of you right now? What is the one step of obedience God is asking you to take this week?

____

____

____

____

____

____

____

____

____

Prayer

Give me courage to follow where You lead. I don't need to see the whole road — only the next faithful step. Amen.

____

____

____

____

____

____

____

SMALL GROUP DISCUSSION GUIDE

Following God's Breadcrumbs — explored in community

This book was written from a place of profound solitude — the quiet of grief, the hush of a hidden season. But the lessons inside of it were never meant to stay there. They were meant to be spoken aloud, tested in community, and received by others who recognize themselves in the story.

Use this guide over six weeks, with sessions of 60–90 minutes. There is no pressure to have all the answers. The point is to show up, to be honest, and to trust that God is already in the room.

Week 1: Impact and Survival

Read: Introduction + The First Theology (Chapters 1–3)

Discussion Questions:

- What impact moment has shaped your life the most? How long did it take before you could name it as formation rather than destruction?

- How do people learn to "brace" after trauma — and what does it cost them to carry that posture long after the danger has passed?

- How does faith change the way we interpret the moments we didn't choose?

Activity: Create your personal Breadcrumb Map using the exercise in this guide.

Week 2: Grief and Time

Read: The Breath Stops / The Stewardship of Silence (Chapters 4–7)

Grief is not a problem to be solved. It is a language to be learned. This week, give the group permission to sit in the weight of what it means to lose someone — and to discover that the weight doesn't crush you. It carries you.

Discussion Questions:

- How does grief change our relationship with time — with urgency, with presence, with the people still in front of us?

- Why do we often live as though we have unlimited time with the people we love?

- What does it look like to hold grief and gratitude at the same time?

Prayer Focus: Gratitude for the people who shaped us — and the courage to tell them while we still can.

Week 3: Identity and Preparation

Read: The Sacred Indwelling / The Hidden Season (Chapters 5–6)

One of the quietest lies we believe is that the years we spent in ordinary labor were somehow off the path. This week's conversation is an invitation to reclaim every season you've ever dismissed as a detour.

Discussion Questions:

- Why do we tend to minimize our own accomplishments — and what does that minimizing cost us?

- What experiences in your life may have been preparation in disguise? What did those seasons build in you?

- What would it mean to trust your own divine résumé?

Exercise: Write your personal highlight reel — the moments of quiet excellence that others may not have seen, but God orchestrated.

Week 4: Relationships and Release

Read: The Reckoning / The Law of Alignment (Chapters 8–9)

Some relationships are assignments. Some are appointments. And some are invitations we were never meant to accept. Learning to tell the difference is one of the most spiritually demanding disciplines there is.

Discussion Questions:

- How do we know when a relationship has run its course — and what does it look like to release it with grace rather than bitterness?

- Why is releasing people sometimes the most loving thing we can do for them — and for ourselves?

- What is the difference between abandonment and discernment in relationships?

Exercise: Spend time in prayer for someone you are in the process of releasing — asking God to hold what you are laying down.

Week 5: Discipline and Growth

Read: The Infrastructure of Care (Chapter 10)

The pain of discipline and the pain of regret are both real. But only one of them produces something. This week, the group is invited to get honest about where discipline has been absent — and what it might cost to keep that door closed.

Discussion Questions:

- What disciplines are hardest for you to maintain — and what does that resistance tell you about where growth is most needed?

- What regret could consistent discipline prevent in your life right now?

- How do you distinguish between rest and avoidance?

Exercise: Choose one discipline to practice faithfully this week — and name it aloud to the group so you can be held accountable.

Week 6: Calling and Courage

Read: Cynthy's Kids / Conclusion (Chapter 11 and Back Matter)

You have arrived at Week 6. Look at who you were when you started this book, and who you are now. This week's conversation is about what you do next — and about the courage required to step into the fullness of what God has been building in you all along.

Discussion Questions:

- What calling feels intimidating — the thing God keeps returning to, that you keep finding reasons to delay?

- What breadcrumbs has God already placed in your life that point toward this calling?

- What is the difference between a calling that feels scary and a calling that simply isn't yours?

Closing Activity: Read the My Divine Extension Declaration aloud together as a group.

MY DIVINE EXTENSION

Read this aloud. Mean every word.

Pause before you read this. Take a breath. Reflect on the journey you have just walked through — the impact moments, the hidden seasons, the grief, the preparation, the pivot points that redirected you toward something greater. Stand in your own unthawed clarity. Then read these words with the authority of a daughter of the Most High.

I acknowledge that my life has been shaped by moments I did not choose, seasons I did not understand, and impacts that once forced me to brace for survival.

I recognize that while those impacts were real, they were not the end. The ice of my past trauma has served its purpose as a preservative, but the season of preservation is over. The season of activation has begun.

I declare that nothing in my life has been wasted. Not the waiting, not the grief, and certainly not the hidden seasons of quiet labor. I refuse to let fear narrated as humility stop me from fulfilling the mission placed inside of me.

I choose a mature faith. I no longer wait at the gate for God to "make it happen." I agree that He has already made it possible, provided the breadcrumbs, and built the infrastructure.

I accept my responsibility. I recognize that preparation does not produce obedience automatically — I must agree to move. I will no longer send the divine call to voicemail. I will no longer hide behind the skirts of my past or the safety of my smallness.

I am not a woman searching for a map. I am a divine extension of the Creator, and I am the map. I reside in Him, and He resides in me.

I am unthawed. I am equipped. I am reporting for duty.

Signature:

Date:

My next faithful step is:

____

____

____

____

____

____

A PRAYER FOR THE JOURNEY

God,

Thank You for the story You are writing in my life.

Thank You for the impact that shaped me, the people who loved me, and the lessons that strengthened me.

Help me trust that nothing in my life has been wasted.

Give me the courage to follow the breadcrumbs You place before me.

Teach me to walk with faith when the path is uncertain.

Remind me that I am never alone.

I reside in You.

And You reside in me.

Amen.

YOUR LEGACY
BEGINS HERE

Not when you arrive — when you align

Every legacy begins with a single decision.

Not a perfect decision.

A faithful one.

The impact moments shaped you.

The preparation seasons equipped you.

The pivot points redirected you.

Now it is your turn to step forward.

What kind of legacy do you want to build?

For your family:

____

____

For your community:

For the next generation:

For the Kingdom of God:

____

____

____

Take a deep breath.

Look back at the breadcrumbs behind you.

Then take the next step forward.

Your story is still unfolding.

RESIDING IN HIM

Where the baton changes hands

"From behind my mother's skirts, I must now stand into the fullness of the woman God created me to be."

— Elizabeth J. Harris, May 21, 2025

There is a moment, a year into grief, when the fog begins to thin just enough to see the shape of who you are becoming.

Mine came on a May morning in 2025. One full year after my mother Cynthia's passing. I did not wake up healed. I woke up with the same weight in my chest that had lived there for twelve months — the same ache of a silence where her voice used to be. And I did what I always do: I picked up the pen. Not to perform. Not to find resolution. But because sometimes you have to say the thing out loud before God can answer it.

I have a dream that one day this day won't feel quite so heavy.

That is not despair. That is faith looking forward. That is a woman who has walked through the fire long enough to know that the fire is not the final word.

And then something shifted. The very next morning — May 21st, the day after the one-year mark — I picked up the pen again. And this time, what came out was not a lament. It was a declaration:

From behind my mother's skirts, I must now stand into the fullness of the woman God created me to be.

I sat with that sentence for a long time. Because I had not known, until I lost her, that I was still standing behind her. I did not know that her physical presence — even at the end, even when she needed care and every resource I could offer — had still been functioning as a safety net beneath me. A foundation beneath a foundation. And when she was gone, I expected to fall.

What I found instead was that the ground had been there all along.

She built it. And God built her.

"I'll never be ALL that God envisions for me, but I'm on the path to fulfilling the greatest vision of myself today. The journey is what's important."

Those words were hers — written in her own hand, tucked among her papers. The woman spent thirty years fighting lupus and congestive heart failure, working, and raising me. And she still found the clarity to write that. The journey is what's important.

My mother handed me the baton on May 20th, 2024 — not because she chose to leave, but because she had finished the work God assigned to her. Her life was an instruction. Her grit was a blueprint. Her love was the first theology I ever received. And I am the carrier of everything she passed forward.

I am in God. And God is in me. And I am whole. I am complete. I am perfect just as I am.

That is not arrogance. That is the sacred indwelling — the truth I had been circling for forty-six years without knowing what to call it. It is what it means to stop hiding from the fullness of who God created you to be.

I no longer interpret delay as limitation. I no longer view my twenty years of administrative labor as obscurity. I have stopped sending the divine call to voicemail. I have stopped bracing for a collision that already happened — and already formed me.

I have reported for duty.

You did not pick up this book by accident.

You have been following breadcrumbs too — impact moments, hidden seasons, pivot points that felt like setbacks but were actually repositioning. You are not a random collection of traumas and tasks. You are a divine extension of the Creator, and the breadcrumbs are already at your feet.

You do not have to chase the light.

You simply have to reside in it.

I reside in Him. And He resides in me.

That is the anchor — and the arrival.

That is where we begin.

CYNTHY'S KIDS, INC.

THE NONPROFIT

The echo of a mother's grit

"I also found out firsthand that grief, like many other types of trauma, can have a way of cocooning you in your own world. You can get so wrapped up in your own trauma that you forget to look up and out to see that others may be hurting, too."

— Elizabeth J. Harris, MSW, March 16, 2026

My mother never ran a nonprofit. She ran a household, a career, and a thirty-year health crisis — all at once, all with grit, all with the kind of quiet excellence that never asked for applause. She did not build institutions. She built people. She built me.

Cynthy's Kids, Inc. is what happens when that kind of woman pours herself into a daughter, and that daughter pours herself into a mission.

We incorporated on February 17, 2026, but the organization was born much earlier — in every lesson she taught me, every expectation she set, every conversation about financial literacy I didn't fully appreciate until I needed it. It was born the night of January 4, 2026, when I sat down and wrote a vision so clear it could only have been placed there by God. Not by ambition. By the God who had been building toward this moment for forty-six years.

Our Mission

The mission of our foundation is to reduce educational inequities by providing scholarships and supportive resources to students from low-income families and historically underserved communities, empowering them to pursue and complete higher education.

What We Do

We serve through three pillars:

Educational Stewardship We walk alongside students through the breadcrumbing process of their own academic and personal formation, honoring the truth that every season of learning has a purpose — even when that purpose isn't visible yet.

Financial Literacy My mother understood that financial ignorance is a form of generational vulnerability. Cynthy's Kids exists to break that cycle — equipping families, young people, and communities with the tools to build lasting security and wealth across generations.

Generational Healing For those in a frozen season: we will offer a place to begin the thaw. We believe healing is cumulative, and that the capacity to serve others grows in direct proportion to the healing we are willing to receive.

How You Can Support the Mission

This book is a fundraiser and a megaphone. A portion of the proceeds from Following God's Breadcrumbs goes directly to supporting the programs of Cynthy's Kids, Inc. If you've been moved by these pages, you've already contributed to the mission in the most essential way: you've expanded the reach of my mother's echo.

To learn more, donate, or get involved, visit: [CynthysKidsInc.org]

Your legacy doesn't begin when you arrive. It begins when you align.

ACKNOWLEDGMENTS

THE COLLECTIVE HARVEST

This book is not mine alone

This book is a collective harvest, and I am deeply grateful to those who stood in the field with me.

To my mother, Cynthia

You were my daily roadmap and my safety net. Your life was my first theology, and your grit was my first lesson in resilience. Your tenacity and your mantra — "If it is not good, it is not the end" — are the very heartbeat of these pages. Your insistence on education, on financial literacy, and on doing it right planted seeds I did not understand until adulthood. Cynthy's Kids, Inc. is not just an idea; it is your echo. Thank you for loving me into ambition.

To my father, Donald

Thank you for the gems of wisdom you placed in my path — for introducing me to diversification before I knew the word, and for teaching me to eat the meat and throw away the bones. For too long, my anger blinded me to what you were actually giving me. I am grateful for the mending, and for the profound truth you offered: "As parents, we do the best we can, in the season we're in, with the resources we have available." That sentence helped set me free. This book exists, in part, because of the permission those words gave me to move forward.

To Mama Blue

You are my second mother — and you have been since I was a teenager. When the relationship with my father was misfiring and my mother was not able to reach me in the way I needed, you were there. Soft. Present. Steady. You navigated one of the most difficult seasons of my young life with the grace of a true angel — never forcing, never flinching, never pulling away.

You are a woman of God in the most unhurried, unperformative sense of the phrase. Your grace surpasses everyone I know. Your gentleness is disarming. Your voice — kind, calm, and soothing — has talked me down from ledges that felt like they wanted to tip me over the edge. I love you very much, Ms. Blue. You deserve every word of this space, and so much more.

To my brother, Joe

Thank you for sharing this history with me. Your presence in my life is a reminder of our shared strength and the roots from which we both grew. Thank you for choosing to do this work with me as a board member and original Cynthy's Kid. I look forward to, one day, this nonprofit and your academic coaching consulting company, Jedai Consulting Firm, will work together in some capacity.

To Uncle Teddy and Auntie Nette

You knew her longer than I did. You carry memories of my mother that I will never have access to — the girl she was before she was my mother, the sister, the daughter, the young woman finding her way. There is something sacred about that. You hold a version of her that lives nowhere else, and I am grateful beyond words that you are still here to tend it.

Thank you for being the family that Mom needed, and for continuing to be the family that I need now. You have stepped into the roles of matriarch and patriarch with grace and intention, and you lead with the one thing that matters most: family first. That mindset is a gift — to all of us who are still finding our footing without her.

To Elise and Madelyn

You are the reason I refuse to stay frozen. You are the reason wealth must be normalized, faith must be embodied, and healing must be modeled. May you inherit not just what I build, but how I build it — integrated, aware, and boldly.

To DuJuan

Twenty-two years is not luck; it is practice, regulation, and choosing each other even when our nervous systems misfire. Thank you for showing up, for holding me when grief pressed in, and for partnering in the volatility of both markets and marriage. You are the kind of man who is never intimidated by his wife's successes — you are the first to push her toward them and have prayed with and for her when doubt tried to creep in. Thank you also for being a living example of resilience, and for refusing to let health challenges diminish your joy or harden your heart. Because you are leading your own nonprofit, Phamily Kidney Lifesavers, since 2020, we understand the weight of the callings we each carry. The calling is too great and the work too sacred for anything less than our collaboration. We will fly together. Thank you for learning and unlearning with me, and for choosing us — every single day.

To Georgianna

Georgie, you are the friend who picked up the phone before my therapy sessions and reminded me that I didn't have to hold the world alone. You told me to stop being the caregiver in that moment and start accepting the care — and that permission was a gift I didn't know I needed. You are in my village, and you helped me learn to trust it. And then, when the time came, you stepped into the work with me — serving as Secretary of Cynthy's Kids, Inc. and making yourself available when it mattered most. You are my A1, and you have been since day one. Thank you for showing up in the season when I needed it most, and for staying when the work began.

To Tenay

You are the kind of friend a woman does not find twice in a lifetime. Our friendship is not measured in proximity or frequency, but in depth and in truth. Some people are seasonal appointments. You are a lifetime assignment. And when Cynthy's Kids, Inc. became real, you made it even more real — becoming an advisory board member and then some, because that is simply who you are. You show up quietly and completely. Thank you for being exactly who you are — and for knowing exactly who I am.

To Darcell

Thank you for the divine alignment of our friendship. You have been so much more than the friend who told me to "get your laptop" — you were the steady, guiding hand for my oldest daughter, Elise, during her foundational first, second, and third-grade years. You have been a teacher to me as well, offering the kind of wisdom and old-school discipline that molds a child into a wonderful member of society. You are the mentor and Auntie I turn to for guidance and wise counsel, always offering your time willingly and with a loving heart. I am forever grateful for your presence in our lives.

To Dr. Wilson

I dedicate this space to you for showing me the way to stay in alignment. Thank you for the powerful example of your faithful leadership and your radical obedience. By choosing to leave a comfortable position to follow the mission God placed in your servant heart, you gave me the blueprint for my own transition. Your yes made mine possible.

To Afua

Twenty-four years ago, you placed the first acupuncture needles in my body, beginning a healing process that started right after the asphalt of 2002. In the decades since, you have been so much more than my acupuncturist and, eventually, my boss; you have been a steadfast friend and a vital mentor. Thank you for being the exceptional woman and practitioner that you are. I love and appreciate you more than you know, and I am honored to have walked so much of this journey with you.

To Dr. Pam

Thank you for helping me understand that frozen does not mean broken. Thank you for reminding me that trauma lives in tissue and that healing requires more than force. You had the hands to reach the ice, and the words to name it.

John, Lori, Sharon, Trieste and the other wonderful host of practitioners who came before

Your hands held me when I was learning how to move again. You prepared my body for the work that would come. You taught me that healing is cumulative — that every practitioner who came before was building something for the next one to receive.

To the FGC Tribe — and especially to Joy, Leah, Stacie, Joe and Dr. Wilson

You are the evidence that when we choose alignment over self-punishment, we create a community that sustains us through the long game. You did not just send flowers; you showed up, prayed with me, checked on me through every hard season, and helped lift my spirit when I did not have words. I honestly do not know what I would have done without you. God placed me at the Fifth Grade Center long before I knew I would need you — and you proved that His timing is always precise.

To Ms. Phyllis

You were one of my mother's friends from her Illinois Bell years — and you showed me what it looks like to honor a friendship even after one of you is gone. During the hardest month of my mother's life, you sent support when you didn't have to, when no one would have known if you hadn't. You were the only one of her early friends who was able to come and stand in that room with us at her memorial. You call me to check in, to remember her with me, and to remind me that her memory is tended with care. Ms. Phyllis, thank you for keeping my mother alive in your heart. It has meant more to me than I have the words to say.

To God

I thank You for the truth that I reside in You as You reside in me — a sacred indwelling that allows me to trust in myself as an extension of Your divine will. You have been preparing me for my destiny this entire time, serving as the steady hand that never let me go in the big scary mall of my trauma and the hidden season of my professional labor. Thank You for not just preventing impact, but for preserving my integration, steadying my breath when my mother's stopped, and warming the ice of my past instead of shattering the woman who carried it. My readiness is the result of Your relentless preparation and the constant reminder that has become my life's anchor: In the end, it is good. If it is not good, it is not the end.

ABOUT THE AUTHOR

ELIZABETH JOANNE DAVENPORT HARRIS

Elizabeth JoAnne Davenport Harris — known to most as Liz — is a builder of systems, a restorer of legacies, and a woman of integrated faith. With over a decade of experience in the education sector — including transformative work at City Garden Montessori and the Fifth Grade Center at Ladue School District — she mastered the administrative breadcrumbs that quietly prepared her for a divine assignment she could not yet name. Her middle name is a cherished honor to her grandmother, one of the primary cheerleaders who helped shape her foundation.

Liz's journey is defined by a refusal to live divided. She has survived the sudden impacts of life — from a flipped car in 2002 to the sacred silence of a hospice bedroom in May 2024 — emerging not just intact, but whole. She is a firm believer that forgiveness is not a gift for the offender, but a necessity for the offended: the act of releasing the weight of the past to make room for the expansion of the future.

As the founder of Cynthy's Kids, Inc. — named in honor of her mother, who was affectionately known as Cyn or Cynthy — Liz is dedicated to turning generational vulnerabilities into structural strengths. Through her leadership at Cynthy's Kids, Inc., she is pioneering a new model for financial literacy and holistic community support in the St.

Louis area, building the kind of foundation she was always standing on — and only fully recognized when she was called to stand on it alone.

Liz resides in St. Louis, Missouri, with her husband DuJuan and their two daughters, Elise and Madelyn. Whether she is building infrastructure for the next generation or sharing a laugh with her people, she moves with the quiet confidence of a woman who knows that nothing in her life has ever been wasted. Her foundation is immovable: God has never failed her.

"I get better and better as I get older. I'm like fine wine, Baby!"

www.ingramcontent.com/pod-product-compliance
Lightning Source LLC
Chambersburg PA
CBHW030430160726
47991CB00005B/1666